THE REVIVE CAFE COOKBOOK 4
www.revive.co.nz

Copyright © Revive Concepts Limited 2014
Published by Revive Concepts Limited
First printing 2014 (this book).

ISBN: 978-0-473-28526-5

Also by Jeremy Dixon: The Revive Cafe Cookbook
   The Revive Cafe Cookbook 2
   The Revive Cafe Cookbook 3

All rights reserved. Except as provided under copyright law, no part of this book may be reproduced in any way without permission in writing from the publishers. "Revive" is a trademark of Revive Concepts Limited.

Produced in New Zealand. Printed in China.
Food Preparation, Styling & Photography: Jeremy Dixon
Cafe Photography: Elesha Newton
Graphic Design: Rebecca Zwitser, Jeremy Dixon, Heather Cameron
Proof Reader: Nyree Tomkins
Recipe testing and proofing: Verity Dixon, Nyree Tomkins, Kjirstnne Jensen, Elesha Newton, Narelle Liggett, Annelise Greenfield, Dawn Simpson, Kirsten Ockleston, Liz Hurlow, Dyanne Dixon, Elisabeth Tupai

The publisher makes no guarantee as to the availability of the products in this book. Every effort has been made to ensure the accuracy of the information presented and any claims made; however, it is the responsibility of the reader to ensure the suitability of the product and recipe for their particular needs. Many natural ingredients vary in size and texture, and differences in raw ingredients may marginally affect the outcome of some dishes. Recipes from the cafes have been adjusted to make them more appropriate for a home kitchen. All health advice given in this book is a guideline only. Professional medical or nutritional advice should be sought for any specific issues.

Metric and imperial measurements have been used in this cookbook. The tablespoon size used is 15ml (½fl oz), teaspoon 5ml (⅙fl oz) and cup 250ml (8fl oz). Some countries use slightly different sized measurements, however these should not make a significant difference to the outcome of the recipes.

Revive Cafes
24 Wyndham St, Auckland Central, New Zealand
33 Lorne St, Auckland Central, New Zealand

Contact Details:
P O Box 12-887, Penrose, Auckland 1642, New Zealand
Email: info@revive.co.nz   Phone: +64-9-303 0420

If you like the recipes in this book I recommend you sign up for my weekly inspirational Revive e-mails.
They contain a weekly recipe, cooking and lifestyle tips, the weekly Revive menu, special offers and Revive news.
Visit www.revive.co.nz to sign up or to purchase more copies of this or our other cookbooks online.
Privacy Policy: Revive will never share your details and you can unsubscribe at any time.
LIKE us on Facebook to get more recipes and health tips!   www.facebook.com/cafe.revive.

the *revive* cafe cookbook 4

Contents

Revive Cafe Update 7
Cookbook Notes 8
Essentials 10
The 8 Keys to Healthy Living 12
Salads 15
Hotpots & Stir Fries 51
Main Meals 81
Soups 101
Sides 119
Sweet Things 139
Flavour Boosters 163
Step-by-Step 179
Quick Guide (Cooking Grains, Beans & Lentils) 186
Cookbook Series Reference Guide 188
Index 190

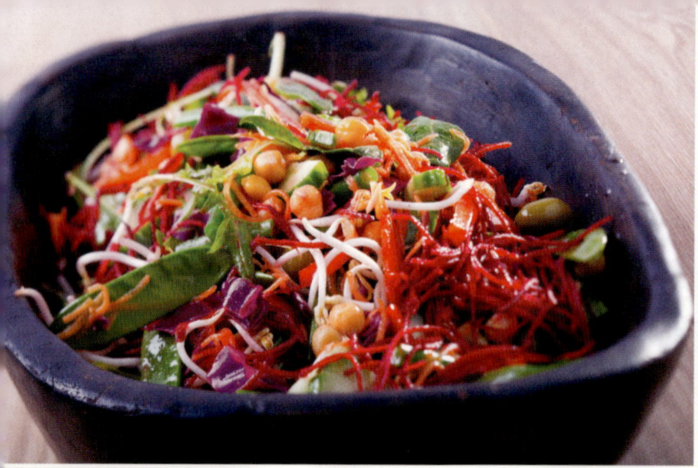

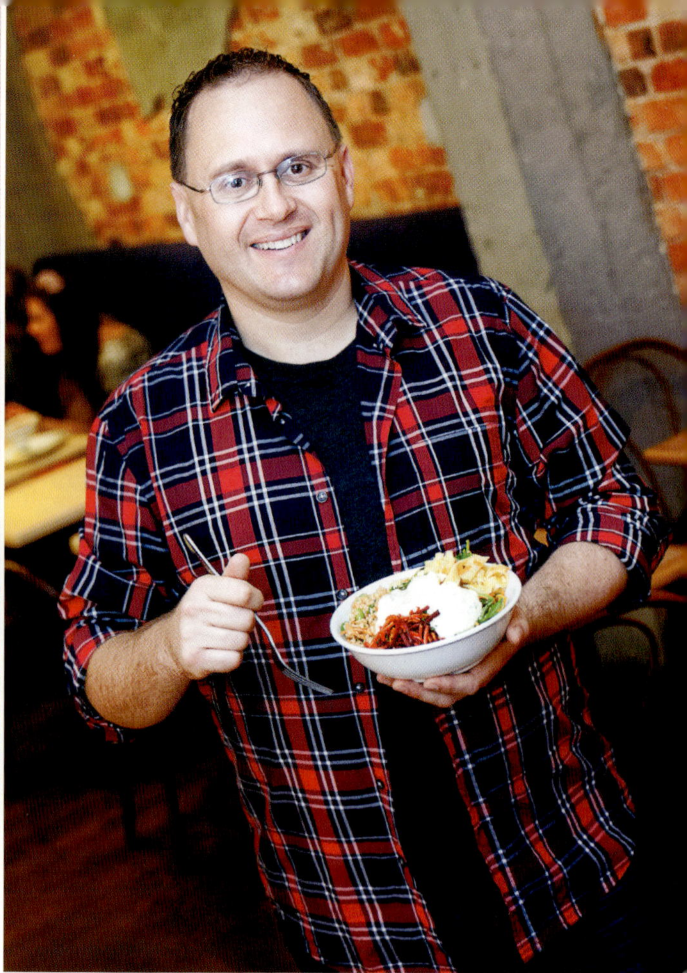

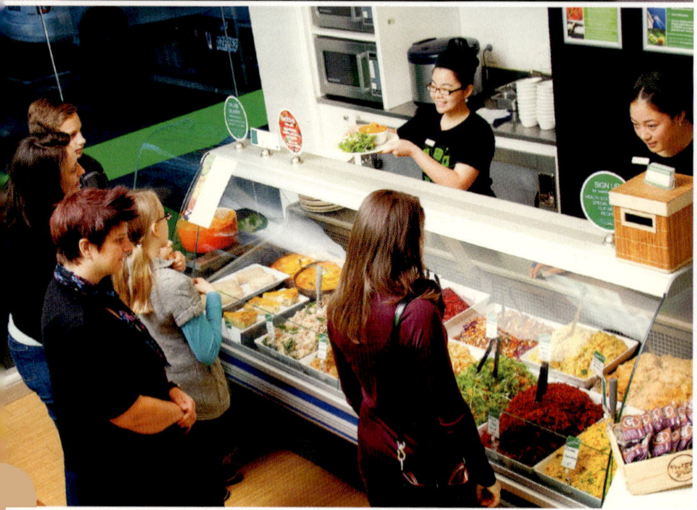

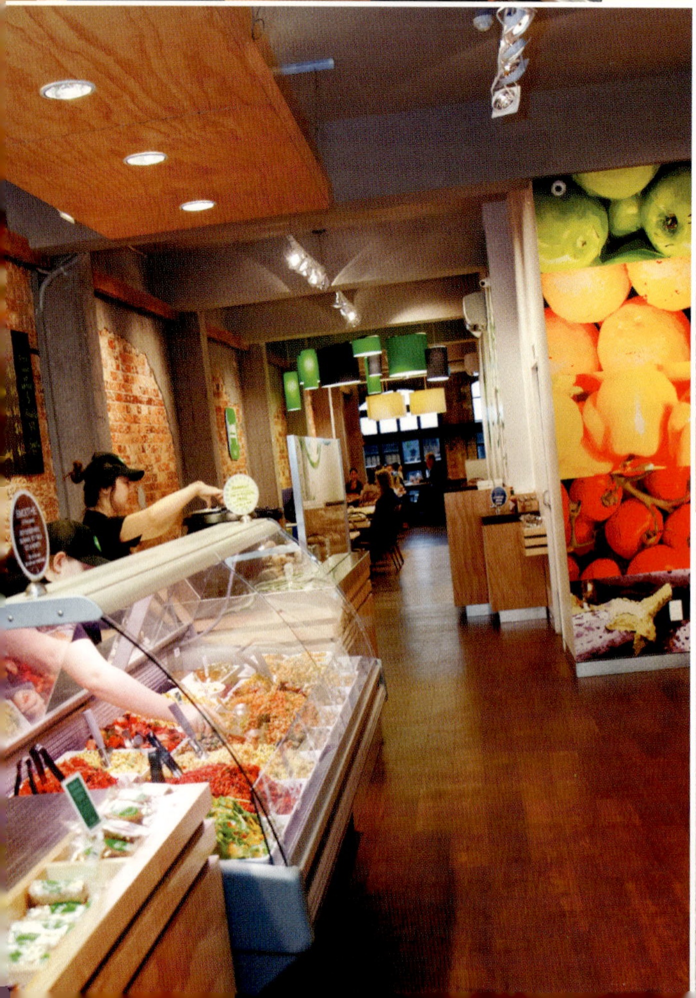

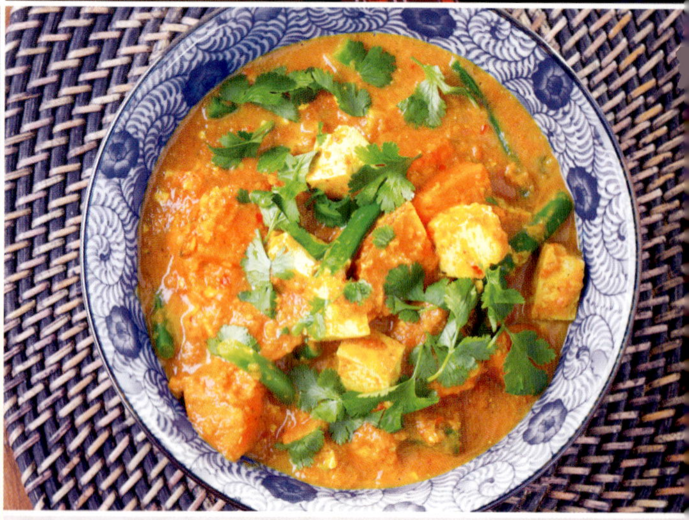

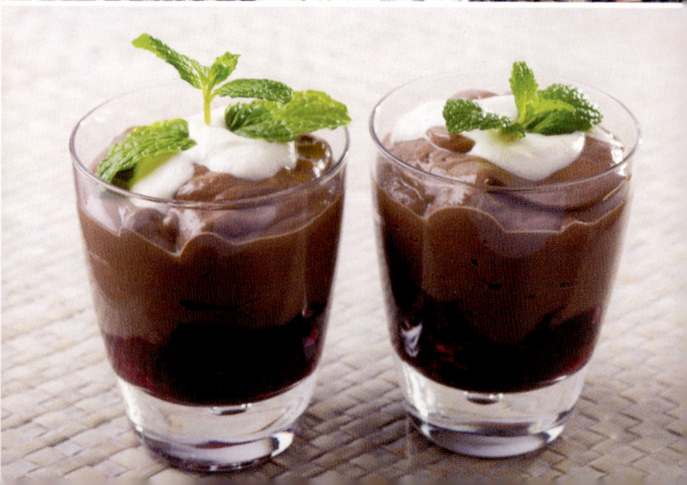

Revive Cafe Update

When I wrote my first cookbook, I never planned for a second book, let alone a fourth. It has been an exciting journey creating so many new recipes and sharing Revive's healthy cooking philosophy with so many people!

People always ask me how I come up with recipes. Even though I have a limited range of ingredients to use, I am finding more and more creative ways to use them. I have also traveled to Nepal, Cambodia, Thailand and the United States in the last couple of years and find plenty of inspiration while travelling. And I love to take an unhealthy recipe and transform it into a healthy one. The healthy Banoffee Pie recipe in this book is one of my new personal favourites.

These new dishes are gradually being introduced to the cafe. There are also many recipes in this book that share the same philosophy and are inspired by the cafe, but due to our current "fast lunch from the cabinet" format are not practical in the cafe at this time. But they are perfect for home use.

In this book I have added a new "side dishes" section - with little quick and easy additions you can make for any meal. And there are more amazing salads, hotpots & stir fries, main meals, soups, flavour boosters and of course everyone's favourite chapter - healthy sweet things!

You may be interested to know that most recipes are developed slowly throughout the year. I experiment a lot at home and in the cafe and when a winner is born, I assemble my camera gear and take the photos in my home studio. I also have a new addiction - collecting crockery. To my wife's dismay I now have 5 large cupboards full of all types of crockery and tableware used to photograph my dishes.

It has been a very exciting year at the cafes too. Our lease on our Fort St cafe ran out on 31 October 2013. This is where we produced food for both the cafes. So it was critical I found a new space in downtown Auckland to move into. In July I found the new Wyndham St site just a couple of blocks away.

After quickly signing up a lease, I had a very busy 4 months of consent issues (it is an old 1900's building) and getting everything built. Fortunately I had a great team of builders and contractors who worked overtime getting it completed in time. We ended up moving in and operating just 3 days before our Fort St lease ran out which meant no interruption (which can be terminal for a food outlet).

The new store is nearly double the size of the old one. We have a beautiful large kitchen with lots of shelving, plenty of bench space, a walk in chiller and space for new ovens and equipment. In the cafe there is a large area for customers to order and a lovely natural area for seating. And to top it off, I get an office instead of working inside the storeroom!

This year we introduced free hummus as an extra to go with salads. This is my favourite way of eating a salad so why not let my customers do it too! We make our hummus fresh every day. Also with my new kitchen I am developing more sweets. Our Plum & Ginger and Apricot Slices are very popular and I hope to extend our sweets range soon!

I hope you and your family enjoy the new recipes in this cookbook and have more energy and vitality with your body loving the healthy whole foods!

Jeremy Dixon
June 2014

Cookbook Notes

Garlic, Ginger & Chilli

Garlic and ginger have amazing flavour enhancing properties and we use both extensively at Revive and in these recipes. Simply chop them up finely before adding to a dish or you can make your own purees by blending the garlic or ginger with a little oil. You can get pureed ginger from most supermarkets.

I recommend that garlic should always be used fresh and never purchased in a puree as it has an unpleasant flavour. You can also buy pre-crushed/pureed chilli in a jar which is used in some recipes.

Sweeteners

The recipes do not use added refined sugar. The most convenient natural sweetener is liquid honey. Alternatively make up a batch of date puree (page 175) which is an excellent and inexpensive sweetener.

There are also other healthy sweeteners available such as apple sauce, agave and maple syrup.

Nuts

Nuts are used in many dishes at Revive and in this cookbook. Roasted nuts are usually used where they are presented whole (in salads or stir fries) so they hold their crunchiness and do not go soggy.

Raw nuts are generally used where they will be blended as they will give a creamier result. However, having the wrong sort of nut will not affect the outcome of most recipes as they are usually interchangeable. You can use nut pieces if you want to minimise cost.

Oils

My favourite oil is rice bran oil and is what I use wherever "oil" is used. It is one of the best oils to cook with as it can withstand higher temperatures. Also, it has a very neutral taste so it is good for dressings. Grape seed and coconut oil are also good. Generally you should not heat olive oil.

Beans/Chickpeas

I have used tinned beans/chickpeas (garbanzo beans) in all of the recipes as this is the most convenient. Drain all cans before using.

If you can use freshly cooked beans they will taste better and are significantly cheaper. 1 tin of beans is around 2 cups.

I recommend that you soak and cook your own beans and store them in your freezer. You will need to soak overnight in plenty of water (they expand three times their volume). Then cook in fresh water until soft, which will be between 30 minutes and 2 hours, depending on the bean and its age. Then freeze them in small containers for easy use.

To defrost, simply run some hot water over them in a sieve or colander for 30 seconds.

Thickeners

I use arrowroot for thickening sauces and desserts in the recipes in this book. You can use cornflour (cornstarch) instead however you may need to use more and you may get a whiter colour.

Creams
Different methods are used to make some dishes creamy. Coconut cream, almond cream and cashew cream can usually be used interchangeably.

Cooking Grains
I recommend that you cook extra grains like rice and quinoa and store in your refrigerator for an easy ingredient to use in the following few days. When you cook grains remember to use boiling water to save time, and first bring the grain to the boil before turning down to a simmer. Do not stir while cooking and keep the lid on.

Cooking Terms
Saute: to cook food on a high heat and in a little oil while stirring with a wooden spoon.
Simmer: to have food cooking at a low heat setting so it is just bubbling.
Roast: to bake in the oven covered with a little oil. Use fan bake setting to achieve more even cooking.

Mixing
You can mix most recipes in the pot you are cooking in or in a big mixing bowl. When mixing, stir gently so as not to damage the food. With salads, mix with your hands if possible. Gently lift up the ingredients and let them fall down with gravity rather than squeezing.

Peeling Vegetables
If in good clean condition, I do not peel potatoes, carrots or kumara. You gain extra vitamins, higher yield and save plenty of time.

Taste Test
It is difficult to get a recipe that works 100% the same every time, especially when you are using natural and fresh ingredients. Sizes in vegetables vary, spices and herbs differ in strength and you can even get differences in evaporation rates with different sized pots.

Make sure you taste test every dish before you serve and be willing to add more seasoning or a little more cooking time if necessary.

Blenders
Some recipes require a food processor (usually with an S blade). Other recipes require a blender or liquidiser (usually a tall jug with 4 pronged blades) or stick blender.

Some hotpots require a stick blender to blend the mixture to make it smoother and more consistent, but if you don't have one don't worry as this will not alter the outcome significantly.

Quantities
The quantities for each dish are an estimate and will vary depending on cooking times and ingredient size. I have used one cup as an average serving size.

Gluten Free & Dairy Free
A large proportion of the recipes are gluten free and/or dairy free. If you have any allergies you will need to check that each recipe is suitable and make adjustments as required.

Essentials Fridge & Freezer

Freeze and refrigerate leftovers and cooked grains/beans. Regularly stock up basic produce as required and as in season.

Freezer

berries: boysenberries, blueberries, strawberries, raspberries

cooked beans: chickpeas (garbanzo), red kidney, white, black, black-eye

corn kernels

peas

red capsicum (bell peppers) diced

spinach (usually in balls)

Refrigerator

aioli (page 134)

almond butter (page 133)

basil pesto (page 135)

crushed chilli (puree)

date puree (page 135)

ginger puree

hummus or other dips

leftover rice or quinoa

relish

soy sauce

sweet chilli sauce

Thai curry pastes: red, green, yellow, Massaman, Penang

Produce

beetroot

broccoli

cabbage: red, white

carrots

cauliflower

celery

cucumber, telegraph

fruit: bananas, lemons, apples

garlic

herbs: mint, parsley, basil, coriander (cilantro)

kumara (sweet potato): red, orange, gold

leeks

lettuce: cos (romaine), iceberg, fancy, mesclun

mesclun lettuce

mushrooms

onions: brown, red

potatoes

pumpkin

silver beet (Swiss chard)

spring onions (scallions)

tomatoes

zucchini (courgette)

Essentials Pantry

These items are shelf stable and generally have a long life. Always keep these stocked up so you can use at any time.

Herbs & Spices

coriander

cumin

curry powder

mixed herbs

smoked paprika

thyme

turmeric

General

tinned chopped tomatoes

chickpea (besan/chana) flour

coconut cream

dried fruit: sultanas, raisins, prunes, dates, apricots

honey

oil: rice bran, olive, sesame

olives: kalamata, black

pasta and pasta sheets

peanut butter, tahini (sesame seed paste)

soy sauce or tamari

vinegar: balsamic, cider

whole grain mustard

Grains

brown rice : long grain, short grain

bulghur wheat

couscous: fine, Israeli

quinoa

rolled oats: fine, jumbo

Beans

tinned and dried beans: chickpeas (garbanzo), red kidney, white, black, black-eyed

dried lentils: red, yellow, brown (crimson), green

Nuts & Seeds

almonds

brazil nuts

cashew nuts

poppy seeds

sesame seeds: black, white

shredded coconut

sunflower seeds

The 8 Keys to Healthy Living

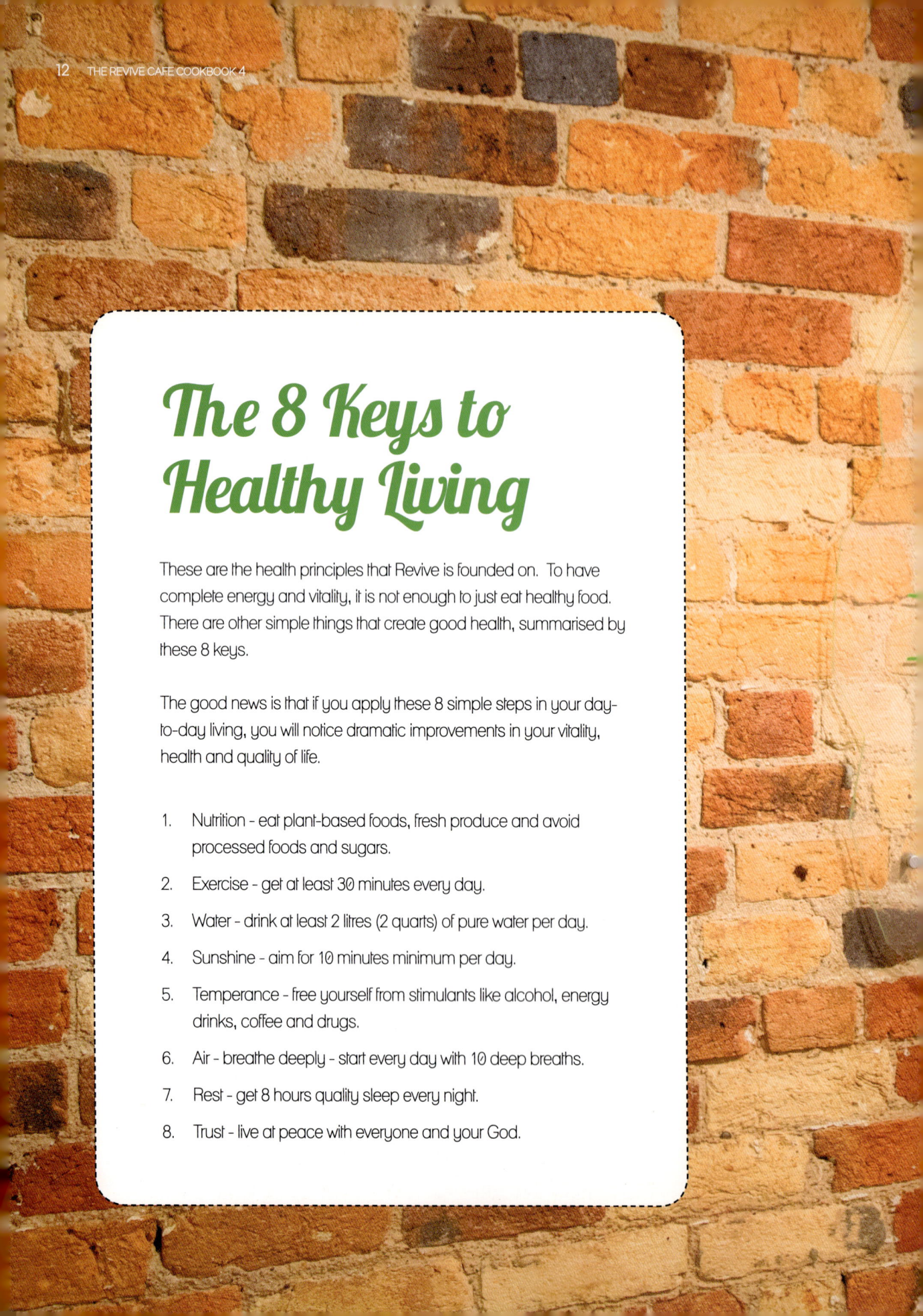

These are the health principles that Revive is founded on. To have complete energy and vitality, it is not enough to just eat healthy food. There are other simple things that create good health, summarised by these 8 keys.

The good news is that if you apply these 8 simple steps in your day-to-day living, you will notice dramatic improvements in your vitality, health and quality of life.

1. Nutrition - eat plant-based foods, fresh produce and avoid processed foods and sugars.
2. Exercise - get at least 30 minutes every day.
3. Water - drink at least 2 litres (2 quarts) of pure water per day.
4. Sunshine - aim for 10 minutes minimum per day.
5. Temperance - free yourself from stimulants like alcohol, energy drinks, coffee and drugs.
6. Air - breathe deeply - start every day with 10 deep breaths.
7. Rest - get 8 hours quality sleep every night.
8. Trust - live at peace with everyone and your God.

THE REVIVE CAFE COOKBOOK 4   13

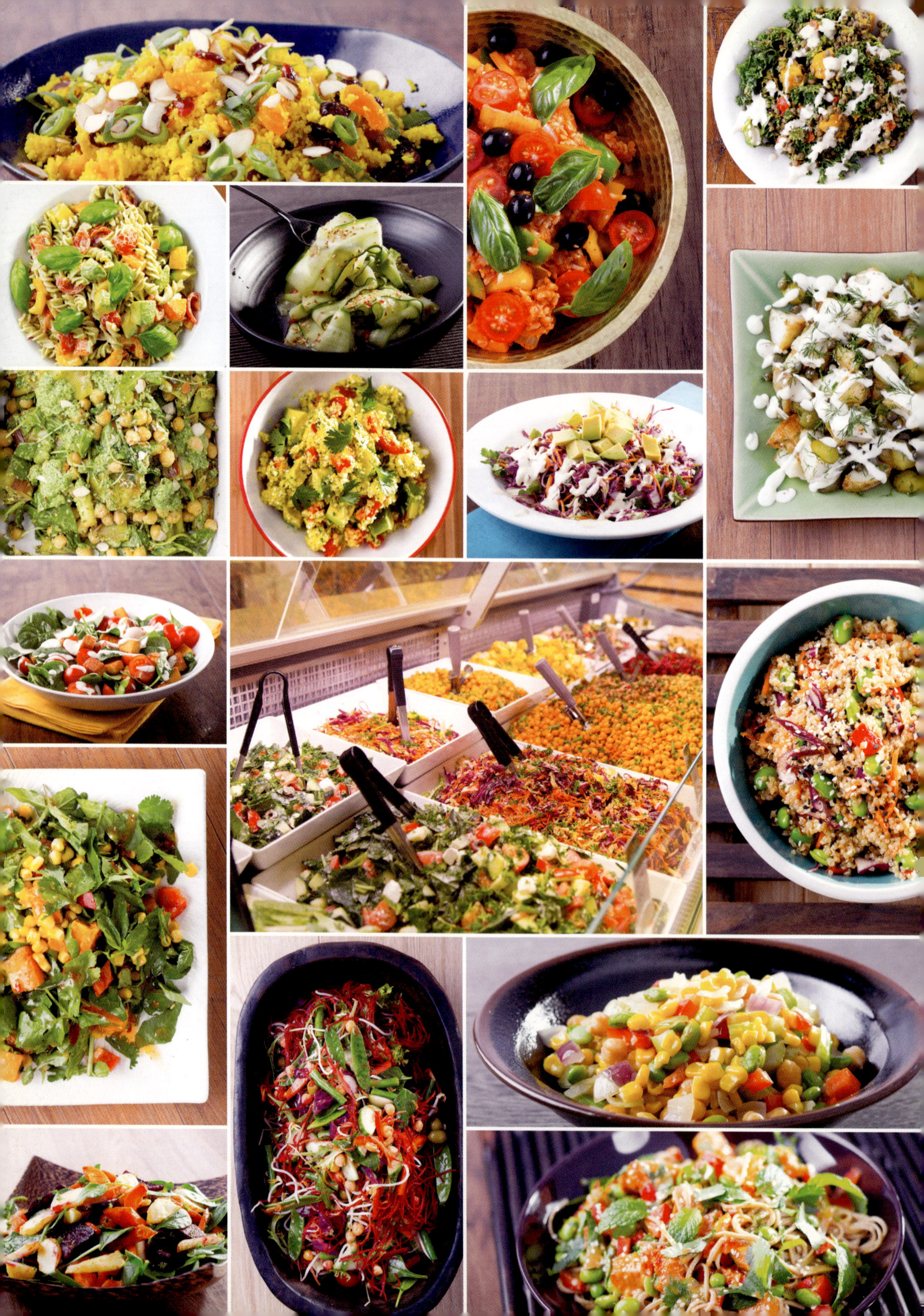

Salads

Fresh Autumn Mingle 16

Asian Quinoa Salad 18

Root Vegetable Medley 20

Asian Soba Noodles 22

Watercress & Sweet Potato Salad 24

Tempeh & Cherry Tomato Salad 26

Cauli-cous Salad 28

Leek & Pesto Chickpeas 30

Kale & Lentil Salad 32

Succotash 34

German Roasted Potatoes 36

Fruity Moroccan Couscous 38

Quick Tahini Coleslaw 40

Italian Tomato Rice Salad 42

Summer Spiral Pasta Salad 44

Sesame Cucumber Ribbon Salad 46

Fresh Autumn Mingle

This is a lovely mingle of various fresh vegetables. Pick and choose your own vegetables in season. The main selection criteria is lots of different colours!

MAKES 12 X 1 CUP SERVES

400g (12oz) tin chickpeas (garbanzo beans) drained

1 cup green beans halved and cooked

1 cup finely grated carrot (around 1 medium carrot)

½ cup mung bean sprouts

1 cup sugar snaps

1 cup cucumber halved and sliced

1 cup red capsicum (bell pepper) finely sliced (around 1 medium)

2 cups mesclun lettuce or baby spinach

1 cup red cabbage cut into chunks

1 cup green olives

½ teaspoon salt

1 cup finely grated beetroot (around 1 medium beetroot)

LEMON DRESSING:

2 tablespoons oil

1 clove garlic finely chopped or crushed

½ teaspoon ground cumin

¼ teaspoon salt

2 tablespoons lemon juice

1. Prepare all the vegetables and put in a large bowl (all except beetroot).
2. In a cup mix the lemon dressing ingredients.
3. Add the dressing and salt and combine gently.
4. Briefly mix in the beetroot and put on serving dish. If you add the beetroot too soon it will colour the salad.

If you are preparing in advance, put clumps of ingredients into a bowl and mix the ingredients just before serving.

Green Olives

Green olives are great for colouring up salads and taste great! While the experts use olives with stones for a more authentic flavour, I generally use olives without stones which makes for a far more pleasant eating experience.

SALADS 17

Quinoa salads sell very well at Revive and this is a great combination. It is my favourite grain. The edamame (green soy beans) and cabbage make this really colourful. This salad is nice warm or cold.

Asian Quinoa Salad

MAKES 5 X 1 CUP SERVES

1 cup quinoa

2 cups boiling water

1 tablespoon oil

1½ cups onion finely diced (around 1 onion)

1 cup carrot julienne (around 1 carrot)

1 tablespoon ginger puree or finely chopped

4 cloves garlic finely chopped or crushed

1 cup frozen edamame (green soy beans)

2 cups red cabbage finely sliced (around ¼ small cabbage)

1 cup red capsicum (bell pepper) finely diced (around 1 capsicum)

1 teaspoon salt

1 teaspoon black sesame seeds

1 teaspoon white sesame seeds

1. In a pot combine the quinoa and boiling water and bring to the boil. Cover and simmer on low heat for around 12 minutes or until the water has disappeared and the quinoa is soft and fluffy. This should yield 2 cups of cooked quinoa.

2. In a pan saute the oil, onion, carrot, ginger, and garlic until soft.

3. Add the edamame, cabbage, capsicum and cook for another 4-5 minutes or until the cabbage has softened.

4. Add quinoa and combine.

5. Garnish with the sesame seeds.

If you do not have any edamame you can substitute frozen peas.

Julienne Carrot

The easiest way to julienne carrot is to firstly cut diagonal slices through the carrot. Then group together 2 or 3 pieces and slice into strips. This enables the carrot to cook quickly and makes for great mouth-feel in salads.

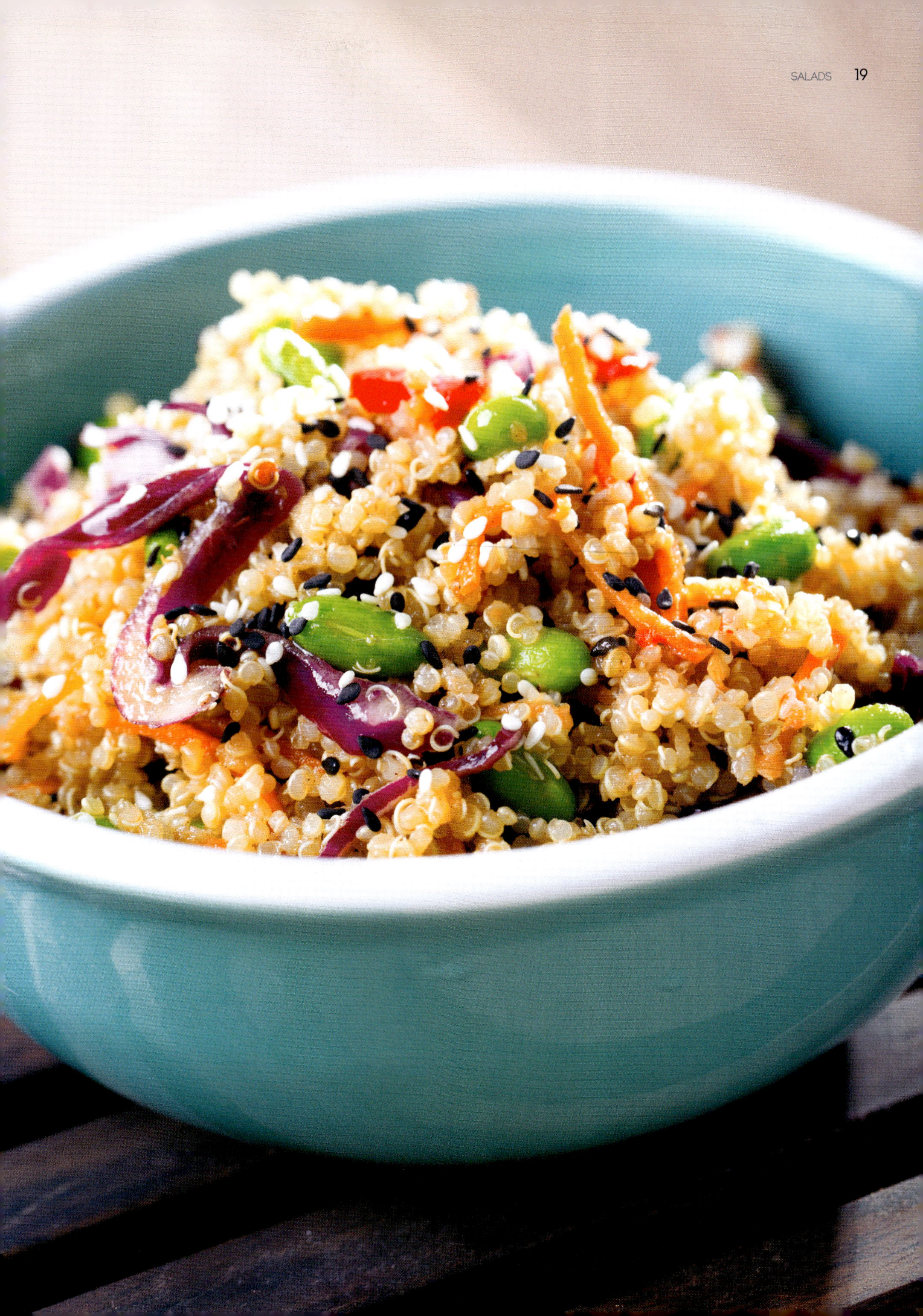

Root vegetables are so sweet and soft when roasted. Beetroot, parsnip and carrot go together well. This salad has no dressing as the roast vegetables with just a little oil and salt are very flavoursome.

Root Vegetable Medley

MAKES 6 X 1 CUP SERVES

3 cups carrot halved longways and diagonally sliced (around 3 medium carrots)

3 cups parsnip halved longways and diagonally sliced (around 4 medium parsnip)

3 cups beetroot sliced and quartered (around 2 medium beetroot)

1 tablespoon oil

½ teaspoon salt

60g (2oz) baby spinach (around 2 cups)

garnish: parsley

1. Mix the vegetables with the oil and salt and put on a roasting tray. Keep the different vegetables separate so the beetroot does not colour everything red.

2. Bake at 180°C (350°F) for around 30 minutes or until the vegetables are soft. Let cool so the spinach does not wilt.

3. Combine gently with the spinach, garnish with parsley and serve.

You can add some lemon juice and/or sweet chilli sauce if you want a little more zing.

If you want some more heat you can add a little cayenne pepper or chilli puree.

Parsnip

This root vegetable is very sweet when roasted. Try it if you have not used it before. Great in soups & salads. Combines well with carrots.

SALADS 21

This is a great colourful salad and you will love the miso dressing. Make sure you include the herbs, otherwise noodle salads can become boring.

Asian Soba Noodles

MAKES 7 X 1 CUP SERVES

2 cups pumpkin or butternut squash chopped into 2cm (1in) cubes

2 teaspoons oil

100g (3oz) soba noodles

3 litres boiling water

1 cup edamame frozen (green soy beans)

1 cup red capsicum (bell pepper) finely chopped (around 1 medium)

½ cup Asian Sesame Miso Dressing (page 165)

large bunch mint finely chopped

large bunch coriander (cilantro) coarsely chopped

garnish: 1 teaspoon white sesame seeds

1. In a bowl mix the pumpkin and oil together. Put onto an oven tray and bake at 180°C (350°F) for around 15 minutes or until just getting soft.

2. Cook soba noodles in boiling water until they are "firm to the bite" or using packet directions. Usually takes around 6 minutes. Immediately rinse in cold water to stop them cooking and then drain.

3. Combine all ingredients together in a bowl.

If you cannot find the edamame you can use frozen green peas.

Soba Noodles

Traditionally from Japan, these are noodles made from wheat flour and buckwheat and have a great savoury taste. They are one of the healthiest noodles you can get as they have more whole grain content. They cook just like normal noodles.

SALADS 23

I love the fresh taste of watercress and this goes well with the sweet flavour of kumara (sweet potato). You may not have tried watercress, but give it a go if you see it in your produce store.

Watercress & Sweet Potato Salad

MAKES 8 X 1 CUP SERVES

4 cups orange sweet potato (kumara) diced 1cm (½in)

1 teaspoon oil

4 cups watercress roughly chopped

½ 400g (12oz) tin whole kernel corn drained (around 1 cup)

1 cup roughly diced red capsicum (bell pepper)

DRESSING

3 tablespoons sweet chilli sauce

1 tablespoon lime juice

3 tablespoons lemon juice

1 tablespoon olive oil

½ teaspoon salt

1. Mix the orange kumara with the oil and put on an oven tray. Bake at 180°C (350°F) for around 10 minutes or until soft.

2. In a bowl, gently combine the kumara with the watercress, corn and capsicum. Place on the serving dish.

3. Mix the dressing ingredients together in a cup and pour over the salad just before serving.

The watercress will wilt easily so reserve the dressing until just before you serve the salad.

You can use frozen corn in this recipe if you do not have tinned. Just soak in some hot water to defrost it.

If you cannot find watercress you can use rocket (rucola) or baby spinach.

Watercress

Watercress has a very fresh peppery taste. It goes well in salads and adds more interest than lettuce. When preparing wash well and rip off the stalks. You can then slice up so it is easy to eat.

SALADS 25

This shows how just a couple of simple ingredients can make a beautiful salad.

Tempeh & Cherry Tomato Salad

MAKES 5 X 1 CUP SERVES

250g pack tempeh

½ teaspoon salt

1½ tablespoons oil

15 cherry tomatoes halved

2 cups baby spinach

¼ cup Tahini Dressing (page 171)

1. Cut the tempeh into 1cm (½in) cubes.

2. In a pan saute the cubed tempeh, salt and oil for around 7 minutes or until golden. Toss or stir often.

3. Combine with all other ingredients and drizzle the dressing on top.

To quickly halve cherry tomatoes, put them between 2 facing plates and slide a sharp knife between the plates.

Tempeh

You have possibly seen this in the supermarket and have been too scared to use it. It is pressed cultured soy beans and comes in blocks like tofu. By itself it does not taste that great. However fry it up with a little oil and salt and it unlocks the beautiful nutty flavours of the tempeh. I recommend you try it!

SALADS 27

I always have fun getting my guests to guess what is in this salad as the last thing they expect is cauliflower. But all are pleasantly surprised.

Cauli-cous Salad

MAKES 8 X 1 CUP SERVES

6 cups cauliflower roughly chopped (around ¾ medium head)

1 cup fresh coriander (cilantro) finely chopped

1 tablespoon oil

2 teaspoons turmeric

½ teaspoon salt

¼ cup lemon juice

1 cup red capsicum (bell pepper) diced (around 1 capsicum)

1 large avocado diced

garnish: extra coriander (cilantro)

1. Cut cauliflower into large florets and put into a food processor and process until fine couscous texture. Do not over process.

2. If there is any liquid drain it off.

3. In a bowl combine all ingredients well (except avocado and capsicum) until you have consistent colour.

4. Gently mix in avocado and capsicum last so as not to damage.

5. Garnish with fresh coriander.

Every cauliflower will have a different flavour and amount of moisture. So test and add more salt, turmeric and/or oil to taste.

Cauliflower Couscous

It does not look like it, but this is just cauliflower crumbs! A great raw and different way to enjoy a "grainy" textured salad. So easy and so healthy. The trick is just blending enough to make it fine without turning it into cauliflower mush.

SALADS 29

This is something I whipped up once when I had to take a dish to a barbeque. The discovery of some leftover pesto in my refrigerator inspired this creation. You can serve it warm or cold, as a side dish or a salad.

Leek & Pesto Chickpeas

MAKES 6 X 1 CUP SERVES

1 tablespoon oil

4 cloves garlic finely chopped or crushed

1 teaspoon fennel seeds

6 cups leeks sliced 2cm (1in) (around 2 large leeks)

½ teaspoon salt

400g (12oz) tin chickpeas (garbanzo beans) drained

2 cups spinach chopped or baby spinach (around 100g (3oz))

1 cup basil pesto (page 175)

garnish: ¼ cup slivered almonds

1. In a pot or pan saute the oil, garlic, fennel seeds and leeks for around 5-10 minutes or until soft.

2. Add the salt, chickpeas and spinach and cook for another couple of minutes or until all heated through and spinach has wilted.

3. Drain off any water if it has accumulated.

4. Stir through ¾ of the basil pesto.

5. Serve and garnish with remaining basil pesto and almonds.

SALADS 31

I kept getting requests from people to have a kale salad. But whenever I tried it I found it quite tough to eat and did not think it would sell. When I discovered it was available at the markets I gave it a go. I was surprised that with a good dressing and some other yummy ingredients it actually tastes great and sold really well!

Kale & Lentil Salad

MAKES 7 X 1 CUP SERVES

3 cups pumpkin de-skinned and cut into 1cm (½in) cubes

2 teaspoons oil

3 cups kale sliced

2 cups (or 400g (12oz) tin drained) french puy lentils cooked

1 cup red capsicum (bell pepper) finely diced (around 1 capsicum)

½ teaspoon salt

4 tablespoons Tahini Dressing (page 171)

1. In a bowl mix the pumpkin and oil together. Put onto an oven tray and bake at 180°C (350°F) for around 15 minutes or until just getting soft.

2. In another bowl combine all of the ingredients except the dressing.

3. Put on the serving dish and drizzle the dressing on top.

For speed I have included using a tin of lentils in the instructions, however they are very easy to cook in boiling water if you have a little more time.

You can use other types of lentils, however they will be mushier than puy lentils.

Kale

A nutrient rich salad vegetable. It is often avoided as it has very tough leaves. However you can make it more enjoyable with a good dressing and making sure you cut it finely.

SALADS 33

My mum used to make this when I was a kid. It is a great combination of beans and corn. It is very versatile as you can serve warm or cold as a salad, or serve as a main on rice.

Succotash

MAKES 5 X 1 CUP SERVES

1 cup celery finely chopped (around 2 large stalks)

1½ cups onion finely diced (around 1 onion)

½ tablespoon oil

2 cloves garlic finely chopped or crushed

2 cups frozen corn

1 cup chickpeas (tinned or freshly cooked)

1 cup edamame (green soy beans) without shells

1 cup red capsicum (bell pepper) diced

½ cup red onion diced

¾ teaspoon salt

1. In a pan saute the celery, onion, oil and garlic for around 5 minutes until onion is clear.

2. Add all other ingredients and saute for around 5 minutes or until everything is heated through.

If you cannot find green soy beans you can use long green beans or frozen peas.

Frozen Corn

A great ingredient to have on hand that will sweeten and add colour and texture to many dishes. Frozen corn is usually cheaper than tinned corn and does not have the additives.

SALADS 35

This is a classic salad that was invented in the first year at Revive and we bring it back on the salad bar occasionally. The dill, capers and gherkins go together really well.

German Roasted Potatoes

MAKES 4 X 1 CUP SERVES

3 cups potatoes diced

2 tablespoons oil

4 tablespoons fresh dill chopped

¼ cup capers

1 cup gherkins (pickled cucumbers) thinly sliced (around 6)

4 tablespoons Revive Aioli (page 174)

½ teaspoon salt

1. Combine the potatoes and oil in a bowl and put on a roasting tray. Bake for 30 minutes at 180°C (350°F) or until soft.

2. Combine all ingredients in a bowl. Reserve some aioli and dill for garnish.

For a lower fat version use the Tahini Dressing (page 171) or Tofu Mayo (page 176).

Capers

These are little olive-like pickles that have a strong and interesting flavour. Good for something different to add a zing to a salad.

SALADS 37

The fine Moroccan-style couscous had never really sold that well at Revive so I did not have it on the salad bar often. I thought I would do my best to improve it so added some great colours and fruit. Now it is a very popular salad.

Fruity Moroccan Couscous

MAKES 5 X 1 CUP SERVES

1 cup Moroccan (fine) couscous

¼ teaspoon turmeric

1 teaspoon salt

1 cup boiling water

1 teaspoon oil

½ cup dried cranberries

½ cup dried dates sliced

½ cup dried apricots sliced

boiling water to cover

¼ cup almonds sliced

½ cup spring onions (scallions) sliced (around 2 spring onions)

1. Mix the couscous with the turmeric and salt in a bowl.

2. Pour over the boiling water and oil, stir briefly and immediately cover.

3. Wait 5 minutes and stir the couscous so it is nice and fluffy and does not contain any lumps.

4. Put the dried fruit in another bowl and pour over boiling water so it is covered. Let it sit for around 5 minutes to plumpen. Drain.

5. Combine all ingredients together (reserve some spring onions for garnish).

You can substitute raisins for cranberries.

If you like your couscous a little sweeter add half a cup of orange juice.

Moroccan (fine) Couscous

The best thing about this couscous is you do not need to cook it in a pot on the stove. Simply combine with equal parts of boiling water, cover and stir after 5 minutes! It has a lovely buttery taste and makes a great salad. You can also serve it with hotpots instead of rice. Try to get wholemeal varieties where possible.

SALADS 39

The key to a great coleslaw is not to overdo white cabbage, or you can even leave it out altogether like this recipe! A nice dressing, herbs and some great colours and you will love coleslaw! The key to making it quick is to use your food processor attachments.

Quick Tahini Coleslaw

MAKES 6 X 1 CUP SERVES

2 cups red cabbage finely sliced

2 cups carrots finely grated

1 cup fresh coriander (cilantro) roughly chopped

1 avocado cut into cubes

4 tablespoons Tahini Dressing (page 171)

1. Prepare the vegetables.
2. Cover with the dressing and avocado chunks.

Use the slicing and grating blades on your food processor to make this salad in super quick time.

Food Processor Blades

When you unpacked your food processor you possibly just used the S blade and put all the attachments in the back of your pantry to gather dust. Get them out and try them. The slicing and grating blades are great for making salads at high speed.

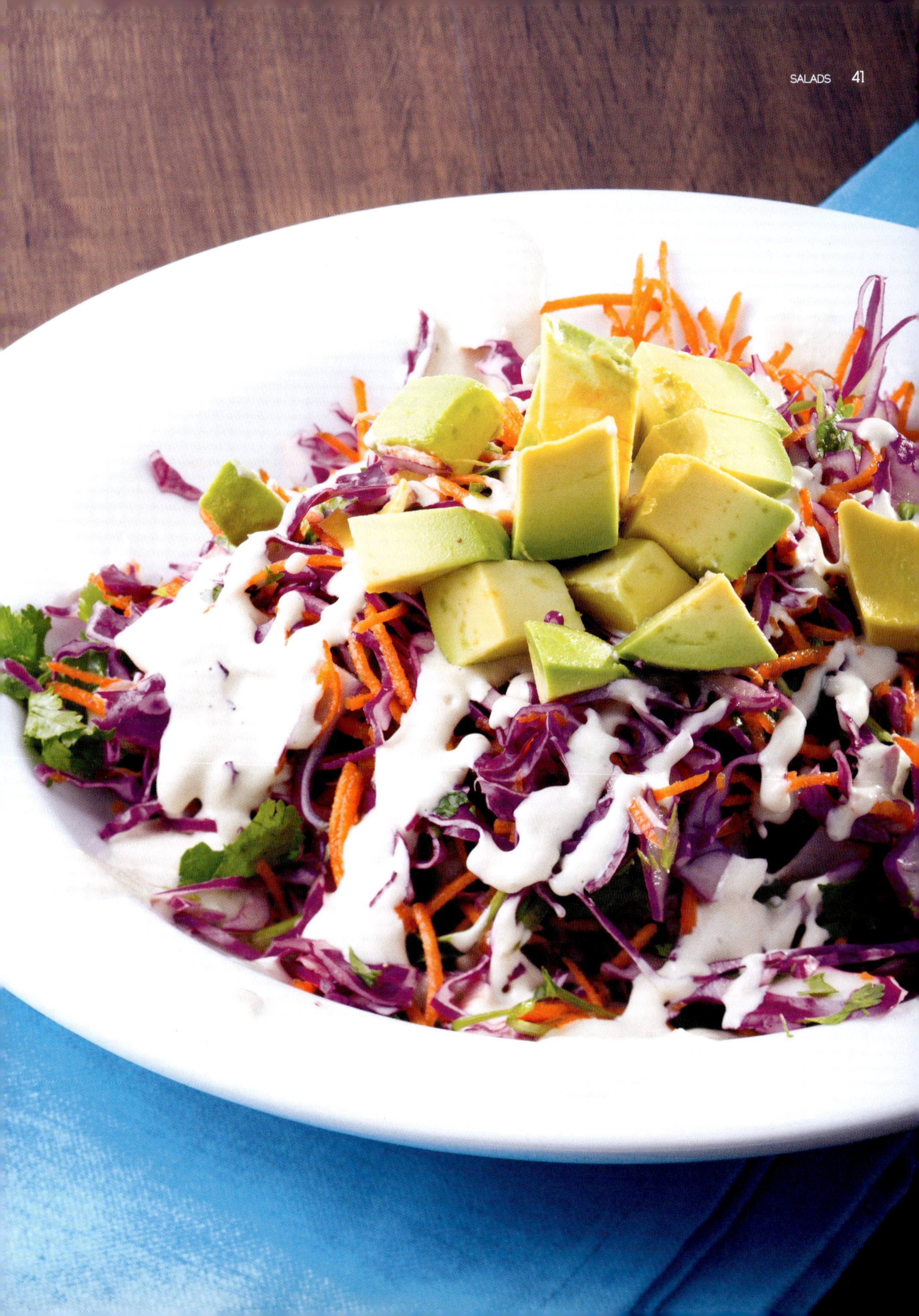

Italian Tomato Rice Salad

MAKES 6 X 1 CUP SERVES

- 1 cup long grain brown rice
- 3 cups boiling water
- 1½ cups onion finely chopped (around 1 onion)
- 4 cloves garlic finely chopped or crushed
- 1 tablespoon oil
- ½ teaspoon salt
- 400g (20oz) tin crushed tomatoes
- 1 teaspoon crushed chilli puree (optional)
- 1 tablespoon honey or date puree
- 1½ teaspoon mixed herbs
- ½ cup green capsicum (bell pepper) diced (around ½ capsicum)
- ½ cup yellow capsicum (bell pepper) diced (around ½ capsicum)
- ½ cup orange capsicum (bell pepper) diced (around ½ capsicum)
- 10 cherry tomatoes halved
- 1½ cups black olives
- garnish: 10 fresh basil leaves

I tried a similar salad in a hotel buffet somewhere and decided to create this version for Revive! I would never have guessed that rice and tomatoes would go together so well. This recipe is great with leftover rice.

1. In a pot combine the rice and boiling water and bring to the boil. Cover and simmer on low heat for around 25 minutes or until the water has disappeared and the rice is soft and fluffy. This should yield 2 cups of cooked rice.

2. In a pot or frying pan, saute the onion, garlic and oil for around 5 minutes or until clear.

3. Add the salt, tinned tomatoes, chilli, honey and mixed herbs and heat until just bubbling.

4. In a bowl combine the tomato mix, capsicum and rice.

5. Serve with the tomatoes, olives and basil leaves on top.

If the tinned tomatoes are chunky, blend them with a stick blender or blender so they are smooth.

As with any salad, reserve some of the colourful ingredients to decorate the top when presenting.

Cherry Tomatoes

These little tomatoes are amazing for salads and usually very flavoursome and juicy. The best part is they stay together unlike normal tomatoes. If you want to halve them quickly, just put them between 2 facing plates and slide a sharp knife through the middle.

SALADS 43

Pesto and pasta always go together well. Combined with some fresh vegetables and avocado this is a great salad. You can also serve this warm as a meal.

Summer Spiral Pasta Salad

MAKES 6 X 1 CUP SERVES

100g (3oz) dry wholemeal spiral pasta (around 1½ cups)

10 cherry tomatoes quartered

½ cup orange capsicum (bell pepper) diced into chunks (around ½ capsicum)

½ cup yellow capsicum (bell pepper) diced into chunks (around ½ capsicum)

¼ cup red onion finely diced (around ¼ small onion)

½ cup Basil Pesto (page 175)

½ teaspoon salt

1 avocado diced into chunks

2 tablespoon lemon juice

garnish: basil leaves

1. Cook the pasta to the packet directions. Usually around 8 minutes in a pot of boiling water.

2. Prepare the vegetables.

3. Mix all the ingredients together.

If you leave this for a while the dressing can soak into the pasta and become dry. So if you are not planning to serve straight away, just assemble all the components and add the dressing before serving.

You can get some lovely heathy pastas made from wholemeal flour, buckwheat, quinoa, corn and rice flour. Try to avoid the white flour pastas when you can.

Orange Capsicum

You can get capsicum (bell pepper) in some lovely colours. I love using orange ones when I would like some extra colour in my dish.

SALADS 45

I love cutting a vegetable in a different way and creating a new dish. Cucumber is so fresh and you can do so much more with it than just rounds and dices.

Sesame Cucumber Ribbon Salad

MAKES 2 X 1 CUP SERVES

1 medium telegraph cucumber

DRESSING

2 tablespoons lemon juice

2 teaspoons sesame oil

1 small chilli de-seeded and finely chopped

1 teaspoon ginger puree or finely chopped

¼ teaspoon salt

1 tablespoon honey or date puree

garnish: 1 tablespoon sesame seeds

1. Using a peeler, "peel" the cucumber into ribbons. When you hit the core, rotate 90 degrees and start "peeling" again. When you only have the small inner part you can stop.

2. Combine all the dressing ingredients in a cup and mix well.

3. Mix the cucumber and the dressing.

4. Put the sesame seeds in a hot non-stick frying pan and heat for around 2 minutes or until they are brown. Shake or stir the pan so they cook evenly while cooking. Sprinkle these on top.

If you do not like hot food you can leave out the chilli.

Peeling Ribbons

A beautiful way to eat cucumber. Simply peel the cucumber long ways with a peeler. This also works well with carrots, courgette (zucchini) and beetroot.

SALADS 47

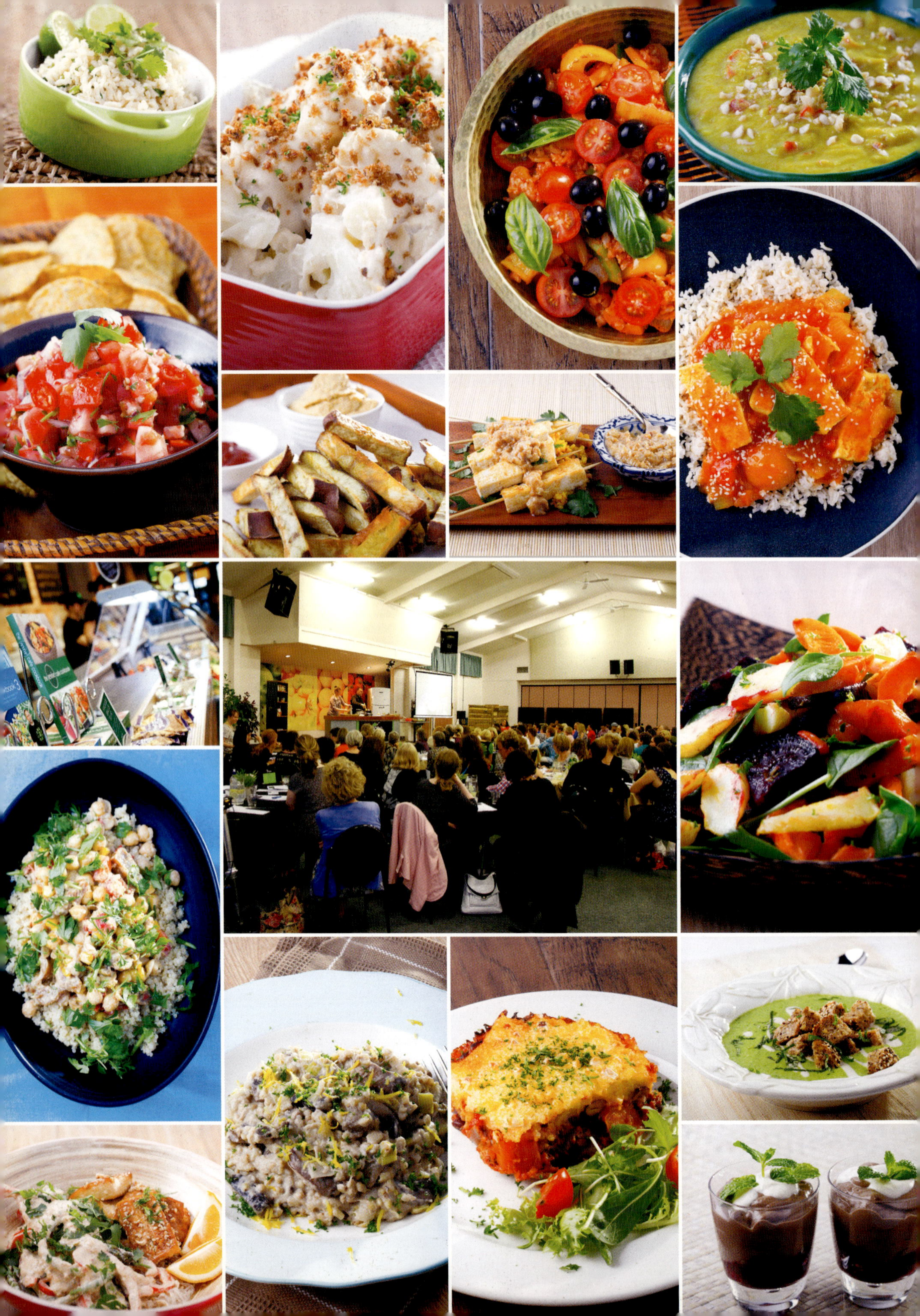

DRINKS
Smoothie of the week
$5.00 or $4.00 with any meal/salad
Sparkling Grape Juice
revive

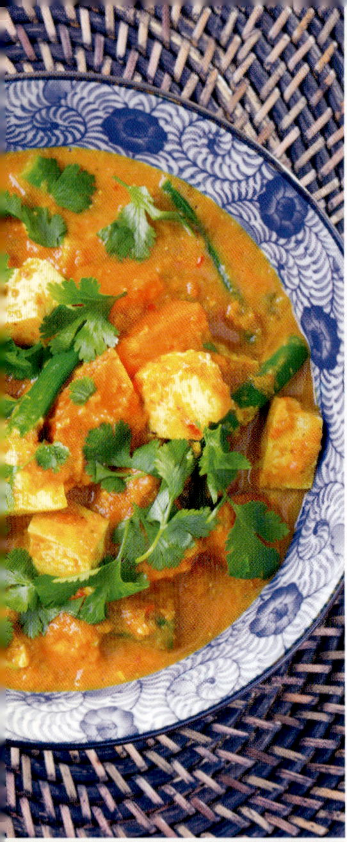
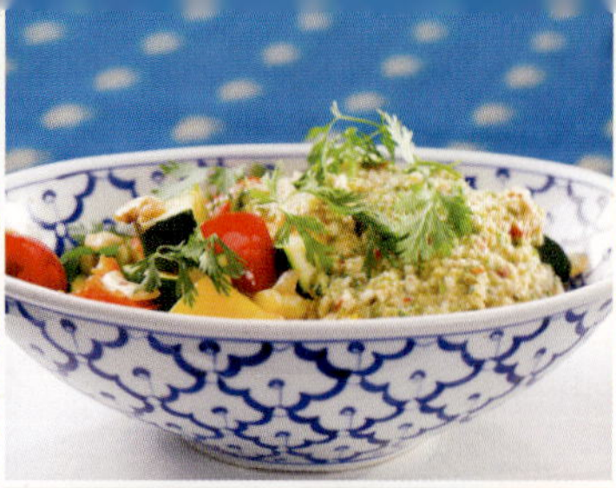
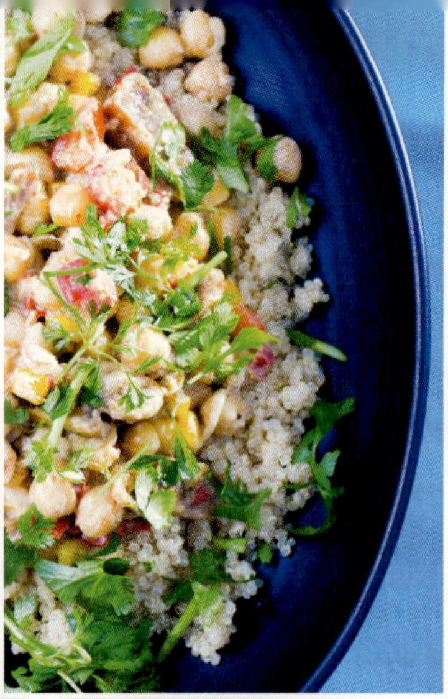
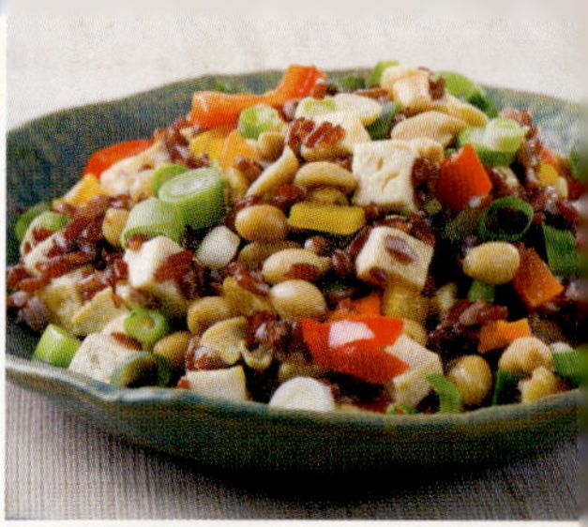
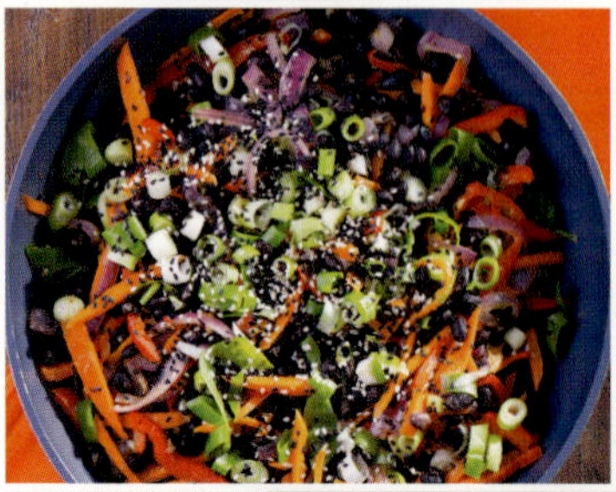
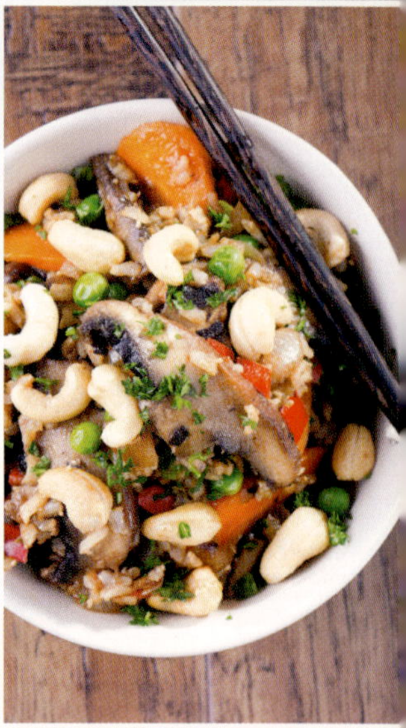
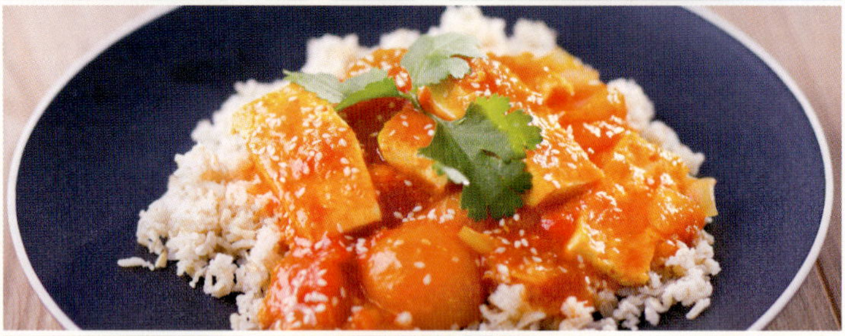
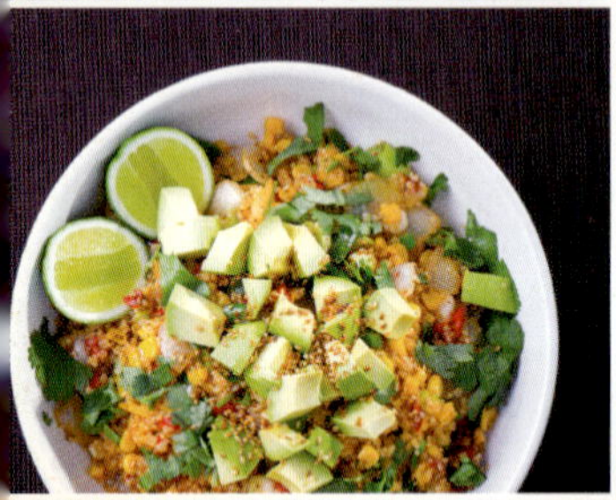
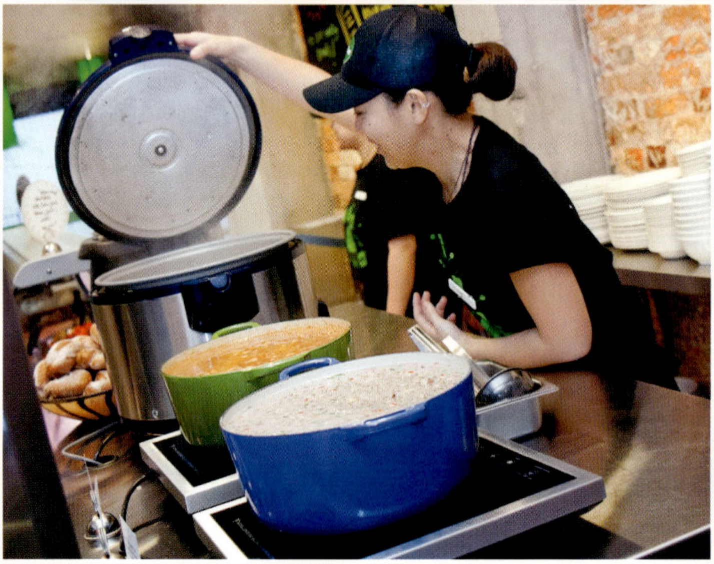
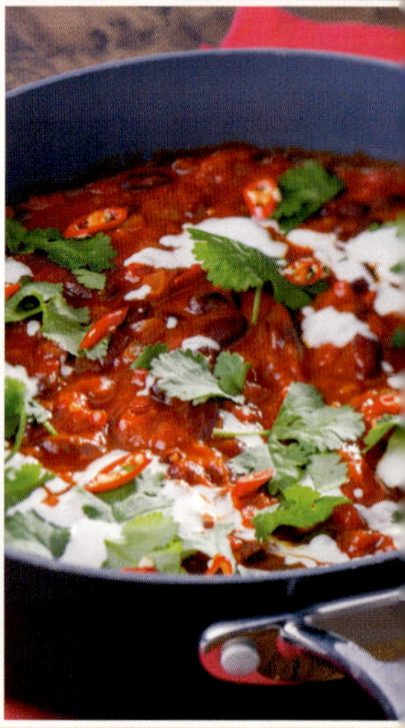
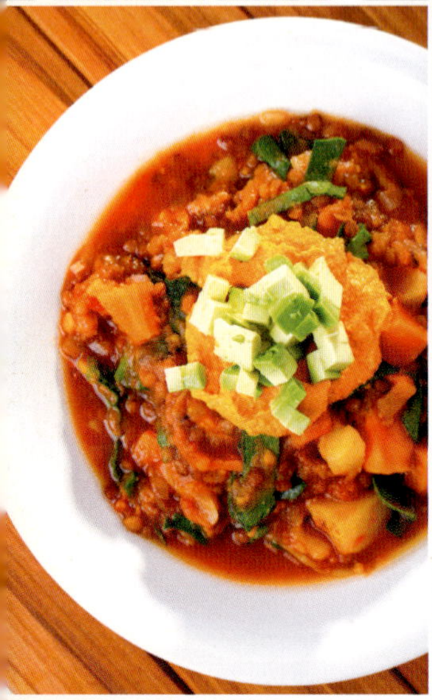
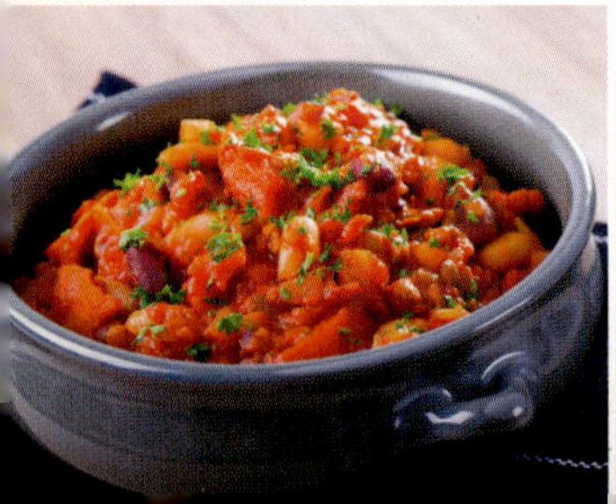
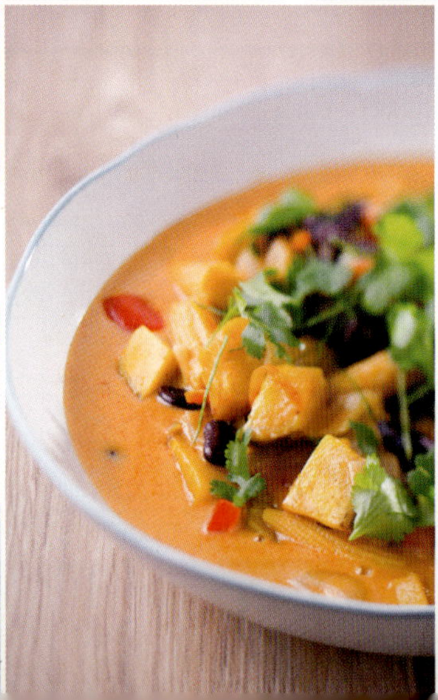
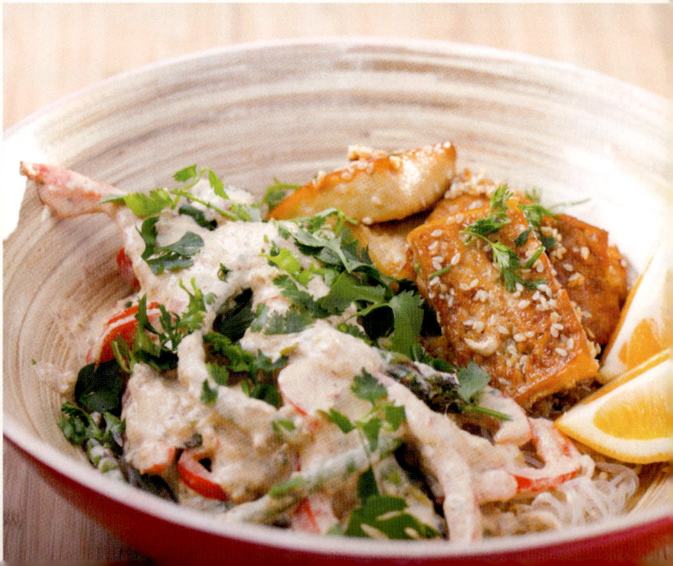

Hotpots & Stir Fries

Chilli Con Haba 52
Aromatic Cambodian Tofu Curry 54
Tuscan Three Bean Casserole 56
Penang Thai Bean Curry 58
Sweet Apricot Sesame Tofu 60
Super-charged Lentil Stew 62
Thai Almond Tofu Noodles 64
Mushroom & Cashew Fried Rice 66
Figgy Thai Chickpeas 68
Black Bean Stir Fry 70
Thai Green Curry Stir Fry 72
Mexican Quinoa 74
Cambodian Red Rice 76

When I tried this dish I was surprised at the fullness of the flavour with the simplicity of ingredients. The sauteed capsicum makes the difference in this dish along with the chilli. You can always back off the chilli if you do not like hot food or have children to feed.

Chilli Con Haba

MAKES 5 X 1 CUP SERVES

- 1½ cups finely diced onions (around 1 medium onion)
- 4 cloves garlic finely chopped or crushed
- 2 cups red capsicum (bell peppers) finely diced (around 2 capsicum)
- 1 red chilli diced finely
- 1 tablespoon oil
- 2 teaspoons smoked paprika
- 400g (12oz) tin chopped tomatoes
- 4 tablespoons tomato paste
- 400g (12oz) tin red kidney beans (drained)
- 1 teaspoon salt
- 1 tablespoon honey or date puree
- garnish: Cashew Cream (page 176)
- garnish: fresh coriander (cilantro)
- garnish: extra chilli finely sliced (optional)

1. In a pot or pan saute the onion, garlic, capsicum, chilli and oil for around 5 minutes or until the onion is soft.

2. Stir in the smoked paprika for around 30 seconds.

3. Add the tomatoes, tomato puree, kidney beans, salt and date puree and heat until just bubbling.

4. Garnish with dollops of cashew cream, fresh coriander and some extra sliced chilli if you are brave.

You may need to stir in a little extra water to adjust the texture if it is too thick.

Tomato Paste

This is great for adding body and flavour to curries and hotpots. I buy a large tin of it and spoon it into ice cube trays. When frozen I transfer to a large container in my freezer and pop out a few cubes when needed.

HOTPOTS & STIR FRIES 53

This dish was inspired by a trip to Cambodia. In Siem Reap we had an excellent curry with amazing aromatic spices. I have tried to reproduce it here with some tweaks. It is a little healthier and I have added some interesting vegetables. It tastes amazing and is now my favourite curry!

Aromatic Cambodian Tofu Curry

MAKES 7 X 1 CUP SERVES

3 cups orange kumara (sweet potato) diced (around 2 medium kumara)

1½ cups diced onion (around 1 onion)

2 cloves garlic finely chopped or crushed

2 tablespoons chopped lemongrass

2 tablespoons finely chopped ginger or ginger puree

½ small red chilli (optional)

½ cup fresh coriander (cilantro) stems

1 teaspoon fennel seeds

½ teaspoon clove powder

½ teaspoon turmeric powder

1 tablespoon oil

400g (12oz) tin chopped tomatoes

400ml (12oz) tin coconut milk

2 tablespoons honey or date puree

1 teaspoon salt

400g (12oz) firm tofu cubed

1 cup green beans halved

garnish: coriander (cilantro)

1. Put the kumara in a pot with some boiling water and boil for around 10 minutes until soft.

2. In a food processor (or using a stick blender) combine the onion, garlic, lemongrass, ginger, chilli, coriander stems, fennel seeds, clove powder, turmeric and oil. Process until very fine.

3. Heat a large pan or pot. Put the curry mixture in and cook for around 5 minutes or until it starts to cook. You want to make sure the onion is cooked and does not have a "raw onion" flavour.

4. Put the tomatoes into the food processor and blend quickly so they are a consistent runny texture. Add to the pan and heat until bubbling.

5. Add the coconut milk, honey and salt and taste.

6. By this time the kumara should be cooked. Put the green beans in the same pot with the kumara and cook for around 2 minutes. Drain the water off and add the kumara and green beans to the curry.

7. Add the tofu last. Stir in gently so you do not damage it.

8. Serve with a garnish of coriander.

You may have to encourage the ingredients down to the bottom of the food processor to blend the curry mix properly. Alternatively you can add a little water to make it blend well.

HOTPOTS & STIR FRIES 55

Tuscan Three Bean Casserole

MAKES 8 X 1 CUP SERVES

3 cups pumpkin or butternut squash peeled and cut into 2cm (1in) cubes

1 tablespoon oil

1½ cups onion finely diced (around 2 onions)

1 cup red capsicum (bell pepper) finely diced (around 1 capsicum)

3 cloves garlic finely chopped or crushed

2 teaspoons oil

400g (12oz) tin crushed tomatoes

¼ cup tomato paste

1 tablespoon honey or date puree

½ cup hot water

1 teaspoon salt

4 bay leaves

400g (12oz) tin red kidney beans

400g (12oz) tin chickpeas (garbanzo beans)

400g (12oz) tin white beans

400g (12oz) tin brown lentils

garnish: chopped parsley

This is a great warming winter dish. You can use any combination of your favourite beans and lentils. And in case you are looking for the third bean in the recipe, chickpeas are technically "garbanzo beans".

1. Combine the pumpkin and oil and bake at 180°C (350°F) for 15 minutes or until the pumpkin is soft.

2. In a pot or pan saute the onion, capsicum, garlic and oil.

3. Add the tomatoes, water, tomato paste, honey, salt and bay leaves and heat until just bubbling. You may need to add up to half a cup of water.

4. Stir in the beans, chickpeas and lentils and heat.

5. Carefully stir in the cooked pumpkin.

6. Remove the bay leaves and serve with a garnish of chopped parsley.

Bay Leaves

Add these to a soup or hotpot for an extra aromatic flavour. Count how many you put in and remove before serving. A starting point is half a leaf per serve. You can also put these in your pantry to help repel insects and other pests.

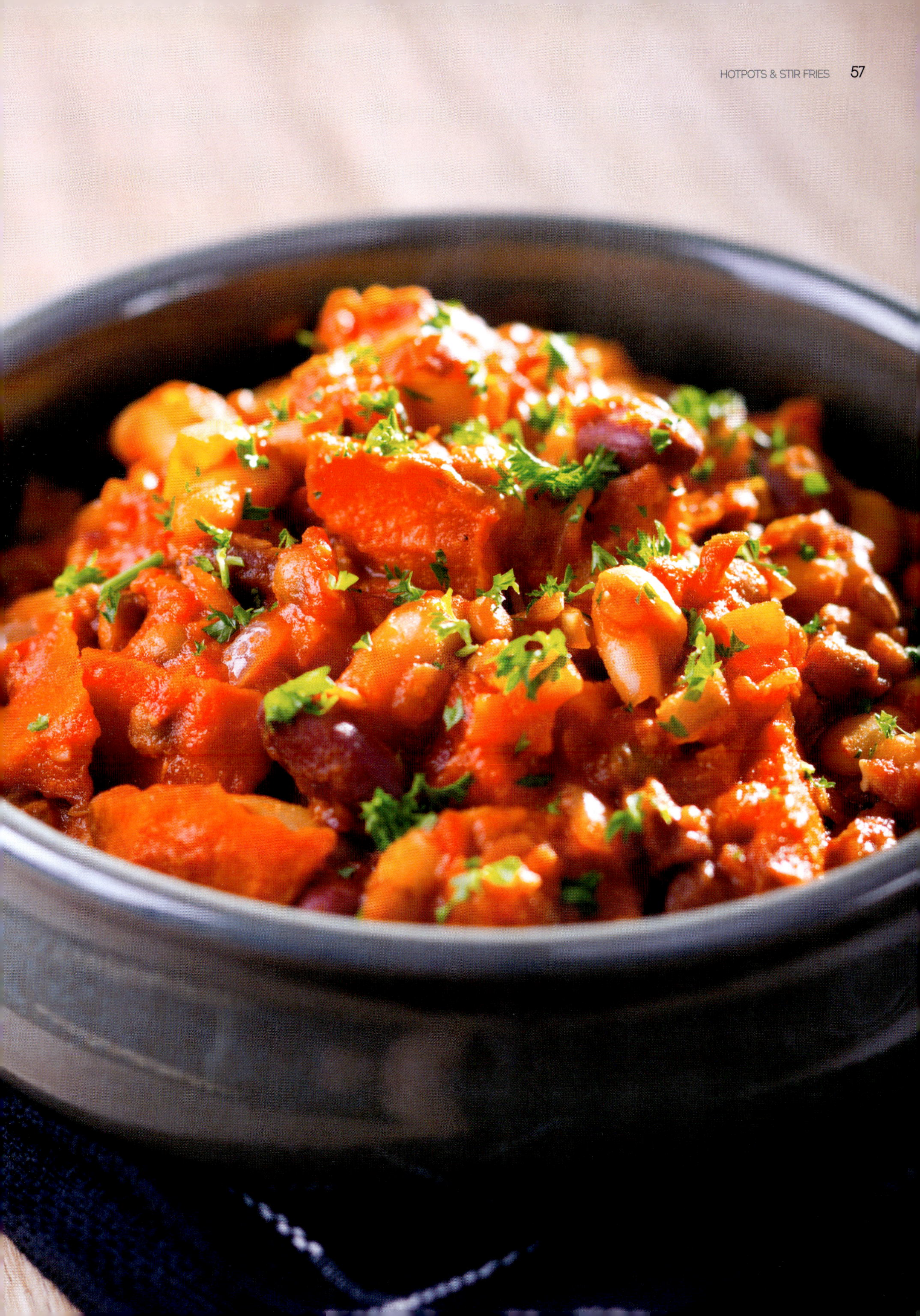

MAKES 7 X 1 CUP SERVES

2 cups gold kumara (sweet potato) diced into 1cm (½in) cubes (around 1 large)

2 teaspoons oil

1½ cups onion diced fine (around 1 large onion)

1 cup red capsicum (bell pepper) diced into chunks (around 1 capsicum)

1 tablespoon finely chopped ginger or ginger puree

2 teaspoons oil

3 tablespoons penang curry paste

¼ cup hot water

2 tablespoons honey or date puree

¾ teaspoon salt

200g (6oz) tin baby corn

400g (12oz) tin red kidney beans

1 cup carrot julienne (around 1 medium carrot)

400ml (12oz) tin coconut milk

1 tablespoon arrowroot

¼ cup cold water

garnish: kaffir lime leaves very finely chopped

garnish: fresh coriander (cilantro) roughly chopped

This is a delicious mild curry. It is really flexible so add different vegetables or protein sources that you have on hand!

Penang Thai Bean Curry

1. Combine the kumara and oil and put on an oven tray. Bake at 180°C (350°F) for around 15 minutes or until the kumara is soft.

2. In a pot or pan saute the onion, capsicum, ginger and oil for around 5 minutes or until the onion is soft.

3. In a cup mix the curry paste with the hot water. Add to the curry.

4. Add the honey, salt, corn, carrot and coconut milk and heat until steaming (but not bubbling).

5. In a cup mix the arrowroot and water and stir into the curry. This will thicken it after a couple of minutes.

6. Garnish with kaffir lime leaves and cilantro. Serve on brown rice.

Depending on the thickness of your coconut milk you may not need to add the arrowroot or possibly add less.

Curry pastes have varying strengths of flavour - make sure you taste the curry and add more if needed.

Penang Thai Curry Paste

The best part about a penang curry is it is the mildest curry paste you can get in the Thai range. So you can add more than usual and get a lot of flavour without the hotness!

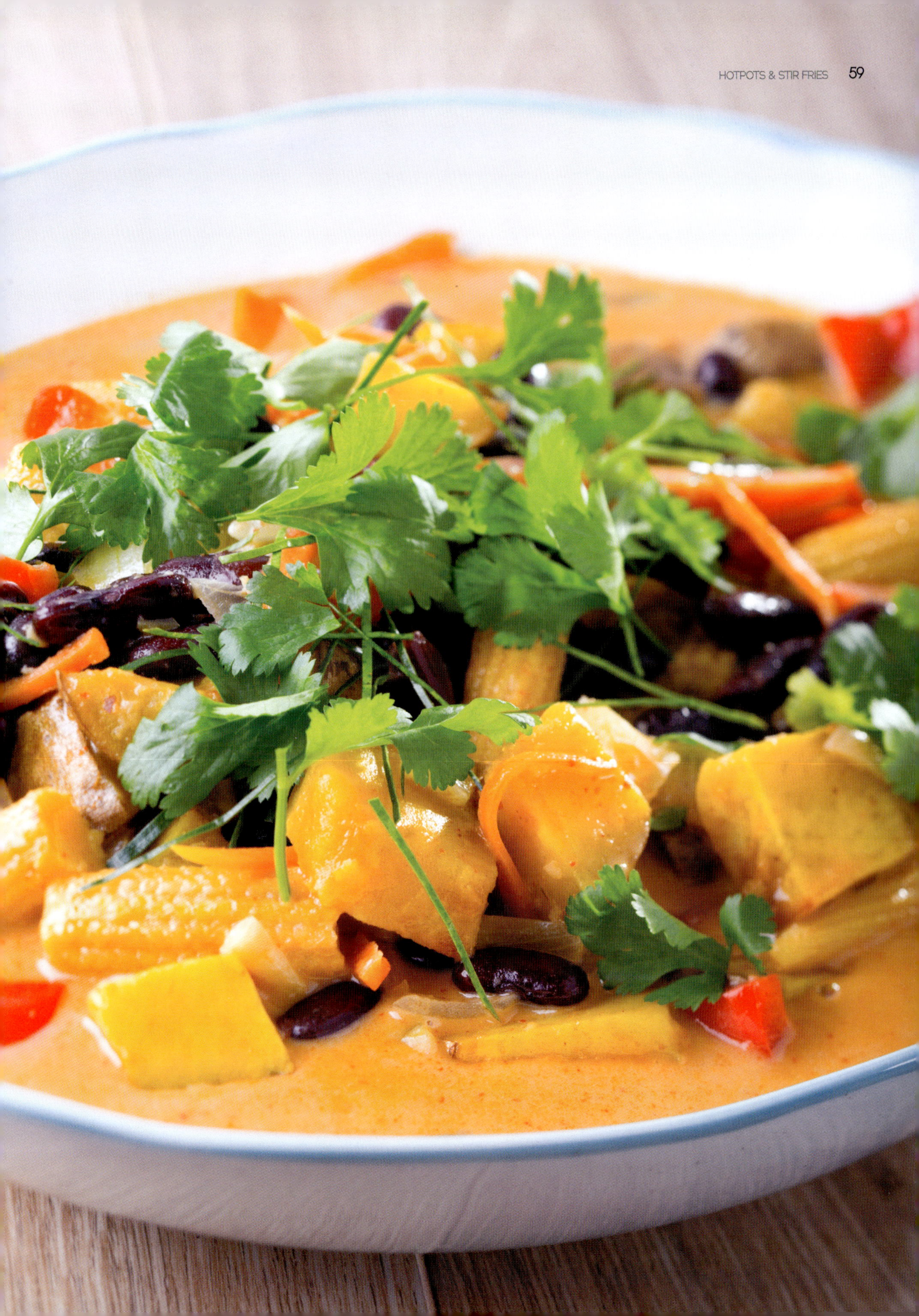

This is a dish that is usually served with chicken. In this healthier version, the tofu soaks up the lovely apricot flavours well.

Sweet Apricot Sesame Tofu

MAKES 6 X 1 CUP SERVES

600g (18oz) firm tofu cut into 1cm (½in) slices

2 teaspoons oil

1½ cups onion diced large (around 1 large onion)

3 cloves garlic finely chopped or crushed

1 teaspoon oil

1 teaspoon curry powder

2 x 400g (12oz) cans apricot halves

400g (12oz) tin tomatoes chopped

1 teaspoon salt

2 tablespoons honey or date puree

2 teaspoons arrowroot

¼ cup cold water

garnish: 1 tablespoon white sesame seeds

1. In a large non-stick frying pan cook the tofu in oil for around 6 minutes per side or until slightly golden/firm. Let cool and it will firm up.

2. In a pot or pan saute the onion, garlic and oil for around 5 minutes or until the onion is soft.

3. Add the curry powder and stir for around 30 seconds.

4. Put one tin of apricots (including the juice) into a blender and blend into pulp. Add to the pot.

5. Drain the second tin and add the apricot halves (whole) to the pot.

6. Stir in the tomatoes, salt and honey and cook until just bubbling.

7. In a cup mix the arrowroot and cold water. Stir into the pot and the mixture should thicken.

8. Carefully stir in the tofu.

Depending on the sweetness of the apricots you may want to add more honey.

Tinned Apricot Halves

A handy tinned fruit to have on hand. Mainly for sweet dishes however it is nice in this savoury dish too. Make sure you get apricots in "juice" not in sugar syrup!

HOTPOTS & STIR FRIES 61

One evening I was making a lentil stew for dinner and it ended up tasting good - but it was not that special and needed something else. I then added some red pepper dip that was in the fridge and avocado to the top and it transformed it to awesome! Don't be afraid to add some toppings to make your dishes more interesting and flavoursome!

Super-charged Lentil Stew

MAKES 8 X 1 CUP SERVES

1½ cups onion finely diced (around 1 onion)

1 cup carrot diced (around 1 large carrot)

1 cup celery diced (around 2 stalks)

4 cloves garlic finely chopped or crushed

1 teaspoon mixed herbs

1 tablespoon oil

4 cups boiling water

2 cups potato diced (around 1 large potato)

1 cup brown lentils

400g (12oz) tin chopped tomatoes

1 tablespoon honey or date puree

1 teaspoon salt or to taste

2 cups fresh spinach

red pepper dip or hummus of your choice

1 avocado finely diced

1. In a pot saute the onion, carrot, celery, garlic, mixed herbs and oil for around 5 minutes or until onion is soft.

2. Add the water, potato and lentils and simmer for around 30-40 minutes or until the potato and lentils are soft and starting to break apart.

3. Add the tomatoes, honey and salt and bring back to the boil.

4. Stir in the spinach last.

5. Serve with red pepper dip and avocado.

You can use any "firm" lentil like french puy, laird or black beluga lentils for this dish.

If the stew ends up being too "watery" you can mash a quarter of the pot with a potato masher and stir everything well so it is mixed.

Dips on Hotpots

Hummus and dips go well on most hotpot or stir-fry style dishes. It can transform a dish from average to awesome in one scoop! Make sure you have some in the fridge or have chickpeas available so you can whip some up with short notice!

HOTPOTS & STIR FRIES

I love having a bowl of food containing different components to combine as I like. My wife will always straight away mix everything very well so "every mouthful has every ingredient" as she says. However I prefer to eat the ingredients separately and combine a couple at a time. This is why these type of recipes are great as everyone is different!

Thai Almond Tofu Noodles

MAKES 4 X 1 CUP SERVES

TOFU:

600g (18oz) firm tofu sliced

1 tablespoon oil

3 tablespoon white sesame seeds

2 teaspoons sesame oil

½ teaspoon salt

2 tablespoons liquid honey

CURRY:

1 tablespoon oil

1 cup red capsicum (bell pepper) sliced (around 1 capsicum)

10 stalks asparagus (ends broken off and then cut in half)

1 cup Homemade Thai Red Curry Paste (page 172)

½ cup almonds

1½ cups water

NOODLES:

200g vermicelli noodles

4 litres (4 quart) boiling water

garnish: fresh coriander (cilantro)

garnish: lemon wedges

1. Heat the oil in a hot pan. Put the tofu in and cook for around 10 minutes or until firming up.

2. Mix the sesame seeds, sesame oil, salt and honey in a cup and spoon over the hot tofu so it soaks up the flavours. Cook for another few minutes until golden, turning carefully. Take off the heat.

3. In a pan saute the oil, capsicum and asparagus for around 2 minutes or until just starting to soften. Add the Homemade Thai Red Curry Paste and mix around until bubbling.

4. Put the almonds and water into the same food processor (no need to wash) and blend into an almond cream. Pour this into the curry and heat gently until all is hot (but not boiling).

5. Put the boiling water into a pot, bring back to the boil, add the noodles and cook using the packet directions or until soft (usually around 6 minutes). Drain.

6. In serving bowls put in the noodles, cover with the curry and top off with the tofu. Garnish with coriander and lemon wedges.

7. If you cook the noodles some time before serving, undercook them as they will continue to cook when they are hot.

If you do not have time to make the curry paste you can use 1 tablespoon from a prepared paste instead.

This recipe can also be served on brown rice or quinoa.

HOTPOTS & STIR FRIES 65

If you like mushrooms you will love this recipe.

Mushroom & Cashew Fried Rice

MAKES 5 X 1 CUP SERVES

1 cup onion finely chopped (around 1 medium onion)

1 cup carrots sliced diagonally (around 2 medium carrots)

1 tablespoon oil

4 cloves garlic finely chopped or crushed

4 large flat mushrooms (around 250g/8oz) sliced thinly

1 cup frozen peas

1 cup red capsicum (bell pepper) finely diced (around 1 medium)

1 teaspoon salt

2 cups cooked long grain brown rice (around ¾ cup uncooked)

½ cup cashew nuts raw or roasted

garnish: parsley

1. In a non-stick frying pan, wok or pot saute the onion, carrots, oil and garlic for around 2 minutes.

2. Add the mushrooms and continue to cook for another 5-7 minutes or until the mushrooms are getting soft.

3. Some mushrooms generate a lot of liquid. A little is good for this recipe, however if you have more than 2 tablespoons in the pan, drain some off.

4. Add the peas, capsicum, salt and rice and cook for another couple of minutes or until all is heated through.

5. Serve with cashew nuts and parsley on top.

You can alternatively use button mushrooms for this recipe.

Garlic Press

While you can chop garlic finely with a sharp knife, it is much faster to use a press. I have a really strong one so I can put up to 3 of cloves of garlic in the press with the skin on and press it through. It works and saves time!

HOTPOTS & STIR FRIES 67

I love figs and I went through a stage trying to put them in every dish I made. I am over this stage now, however I did create this dish one night and it tastes great.

Figgy Thai Chickpeas

MAKES 5 X 1 CUP SERVES

10 dried figs

2 cups boiling water

1 teaspoon oil

1 cup red capsicum (bell pepper) diced finely (around 1 capsicum)

1 cup frozen corn

1 tablespoon Thai red curry paste

2 x 400g (12oz) tins chickpeas (garbanzo beans) (or 4 cups cooked)

½ teaspoon salt

½ cup coconut cream

garnish: fresh coriander (cilantro)

serve with: cooked quinoa or brown rice

1. Slice the figs into ½cm (¼in) strips and soak in a bowl with boiling water for around 5 minutes.

2. In a large pot or pan saute the oil, capsicum and corn for around 3 minutes or until starting to get soft.

3. Add the curry paste and heat. You may need to add a little water.

4. Add the chickpeas, salt, coconut cream and drained figs and stir until hot (but not boiling).

5. Serve over cooked quinoa or brown rice and garnish with fresh coriander.

Freezing Chickpeas

Every couple of months I will soak and cook a large pot of chickpeas. When cooked I put them into used Revive salad containers and put them in the freezer. Whenever I need chickpeas for a hotpot (or to make hummus) I take a container out, run hot water over it for about 30 seconds and they are ready to use!

HOTPOTS & STIR FRIES 69

While I was on a trip in Cambodia I demonstrated some recipes to the locals. They are very short of protein yet have a vast array of beans available to them. The only issue is that in Asia, beans are associated with sweet dishes, not savoury. So I showed them how to make this tasty stir-fry with black beans and also to get as many different colours as possible into their cooking.

Black Bean Stir Fry

MAKES 3 X 1 CUP SERVES

1 tablespoon oil

2 cloves garlic finely chopped or crushed

1½ cups red onion sliced (1 large onion)

1 cup red capsicum (bell pepper) sliced thinly (around 1 capsicum)

1 cup carrot julienne (around 1 medium carrot)

1 tablespoon finely chopped ginger or ginger puree

4 cloves garlic

400g (12oz) tin black beans (drained)

1 tablespoon honey

1 teaspoon salt

1 teaspoon black sesame seeds

1 teaspoon white sesame seeds

2 tablespoons lime juice (around 1 lime)

1 large spring onion (scallions) sliced

1. In a pan saute the oil, garlic, onion, peppers, carrots, ginger and garlic for around 5 minutes or until onion is soft.

2. Add the black beans, honey and salt and heat while stirring gently for another 3 minutes or until everything is cooked (but still firm).

3. Garnish with sesame seeds, lime juice and spring onions and serve.

HOTPOTS & STIR FRIES 71

This is a quick and easy way to have a tasty stir fry with a pour-over coconut curry!!!

Thai Green Curry Stir Fry

MAKES 6 X 1 CUP SERVES

1 tablespoon oil

1 cup red capsicum (bell pepper) 2cm (1in) diced (around 1 capsicum)

1 cup yellow capsicum (bell pepper) 2cm (1in) diced (around 1 capsicum)

2 cups courgette (zucchini) 2cm (1in) diced (around 1 courgette)

1½ cups onion diced 1cm (½in) (around 1 onion)

½ teaspoon salt

1 cup Homemade Thai Green Curry Paste (page 173)

200ml (6oz) coconut milk

½ cup cashew nuts raw

garnish: fresh coriander (cilantro)

1. In a pot or pan saute the oil, capsicum, courgette and onion for around 5 minutes or until soft. Add the salt.

2. In another pan heat the curry paste until hot and add the coconut milk.

3. In a small pan cook the cashew nuts (without oil) until browned. Add to the vegetable mix.

4. Serve the vegetables with the curry paste poured over the top and coriander for garnish.

Coconut Milk

This is a great creamy ingredient to make curries and stir fries awesome! Coconut milk comes from the flesh of the coconut and is combined and squeezed with water to produce a lovely milk. Coconut cream is produced in the same way, just with less water, and ends up being thicker.

HOTPOTS & STIR FRIES 73

I made this for dinner one night in a hurry, slapping together leftover ingredients from the fridge and freezer. I expected it to taste okay, but when I tasted it, I was surprised how amazing it was!!! So I had to include it in this book! The celery seeds, fresh coriander and lime juice give it an amazing tangy flavour.

Mexican Quinoa

MAKES 6 X 1 CUP SERVES

- ½ cup quinoa
- 1 cup boiling water
- 1½ cups onion diced (around 1 onion)
- 4 cloves garlic finely chopped or crushed
- 1 cup red capsicum (bell pepper) finely diced (around 1 large)
- 1 tablespoon oil
- 2 cups corn frozen
- 1 tablespoon celery seeds
- ½ teaspoon salt
- 2 tablespoons toasted sesame seeds
- ½ cup spring onions (scallions) sliced
- 1 cup coriander (cilantro) roughly chopped
- 1 avocado diced
- ¼ cup lime juice (around 2 limes)

1. In a pot combine the quinoa and boiling water and bring to the boil. Cover and simmer on low heat for around 12 minutes or until the water has disappeared and the quinoa is soft and fluffy. This should yield 1½ cups of cooked quinoa.

2. Saute the onion, garlic, capsicum and oil for around 5 minutes or until the onion is soft.

3. Add the corn, quinoa, celery seeds and salt. Cook for another 3-4 minutes or until everything is hot.

4. Put the sesame seeds in a hot non-stick frying pan and heat for around 2 minutes or until they are brown. Shake or stir the pan so they cook evenly while cooking. Sprinkle these on top.

5. Serve topped with the sesame seeds, spring onions, coriander and avocado. Drizzle over the lime juice.

You can add some chilli or chilli puree to this dish if you like hot food.

Celery Seeds

These give fresh bursts of tangy flavour and are a great surprise ingredient to add to salads and stir fries. You may not find them in mainstream supermarkets, however most bulk bin or whole food stores generally stock them.

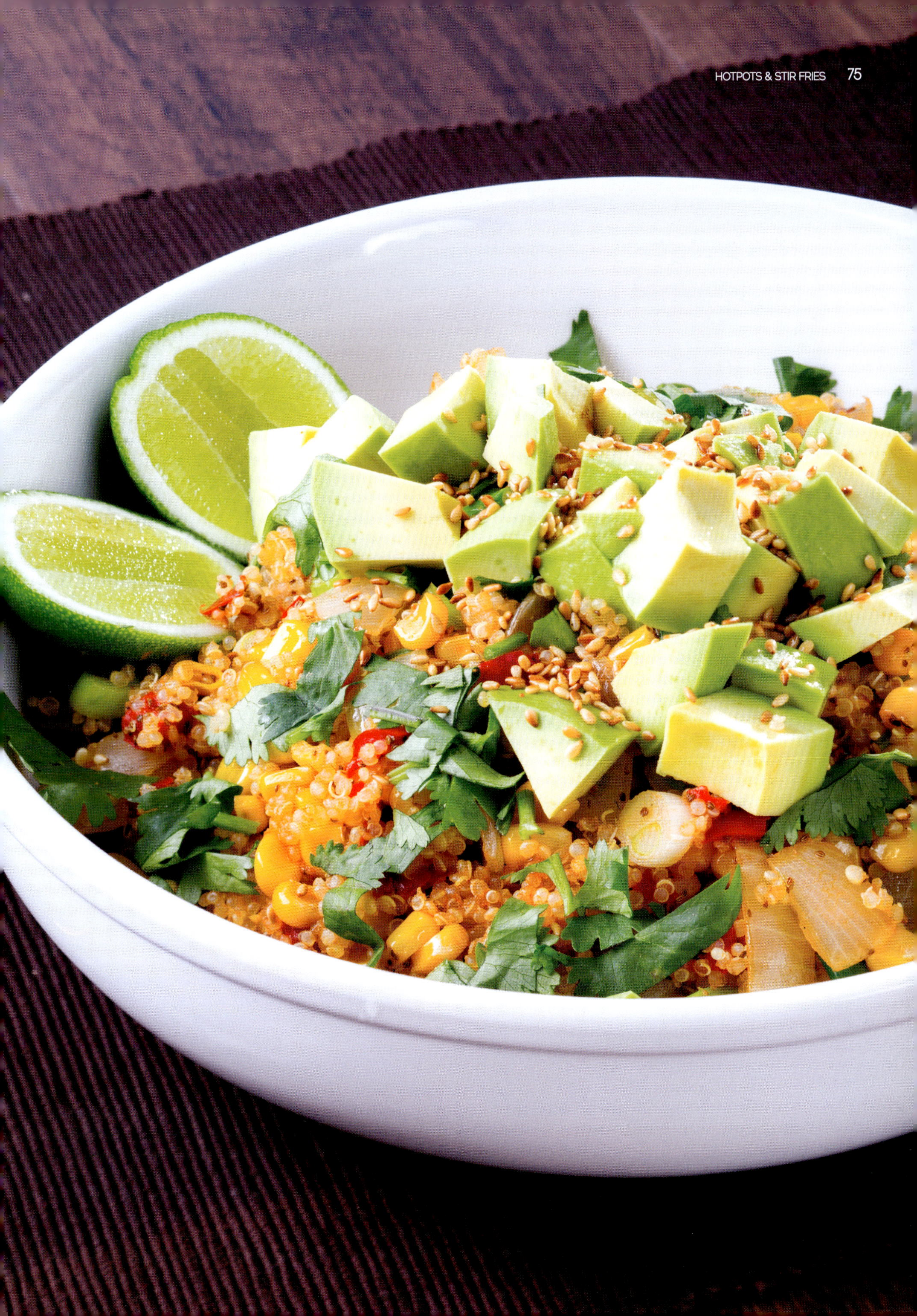

When visiting Cambodia, we arranged a bag of brown rice so our hotel could supply us with healthy meals and lunches. For some reason they ordered red rice instead, and they made a stir fry for our lunch each day that inspired this dish. It was delicious for the first day, however after 5 days of the same thing the novelty did wear off. Here is my version of it with some extra flavour and more "goodies-to-rice" ratio.

Cambodian Red Rice

MAKES 7 X 1 CUP SERVES

¾ cup red rice

1½ cups boiling water

2 tablespoons oil

340g (10oz) firm tofu cubed small

½ cup red capsicum (bell pepper) diced (around 1 capsicum)

½ cup green capsicum (bell pepper) diced (around 1 capsicum)

½ cup yellow capsicum (bell pepper) diced (around 1 capsicum)

1 teaspoon salt

1 cup roasted peanuts

1 cup spring onions (scallions) finely sliced (around 2 stalks)

1. In a pot combine the rice and boiling water and bring to the boil. Cover and simmer on low heat for around 30 minutes or until the water has disappeared and the rice is soft and fluffy. This should yield 2 cups of cooked rice.

2. In a non-stick frying pan saute the tofu with the oil until the tofu has firmed up and browned a little. Stir gently and make sure the tofu does not stick to the pan.

3. Add the capsicum, salt and peanuts. Saute for around 5 minutes or until all has heated through.

4. Stir in the cooked rice and spring onions and mix gently.

Red Rice

A beautiful coloured rice you can use in stir fries for more colour and texture. It is harder to eat so you would not generally serve a hotpot over it though. Cooks the same as brown rice but can take a little longer.

HOTPOTS & STIR FRIES 77

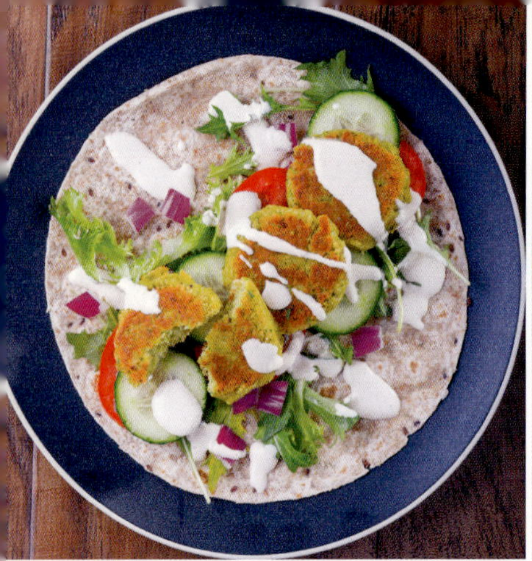
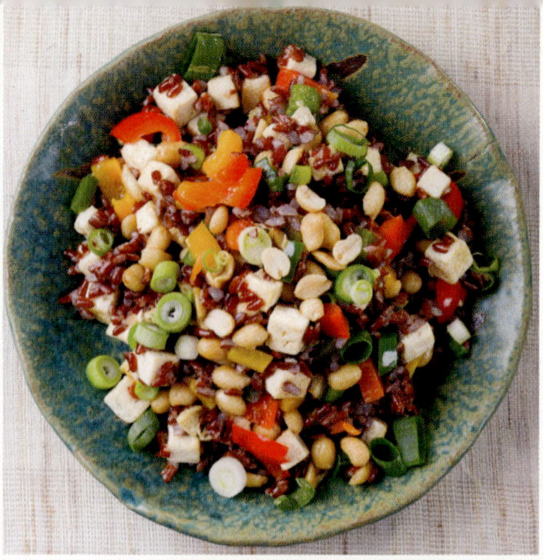
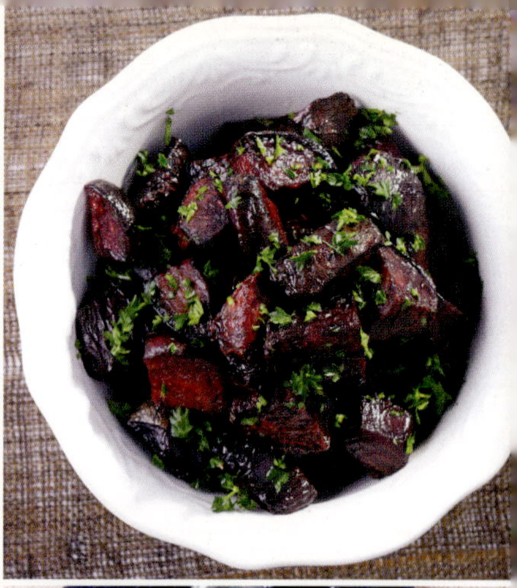
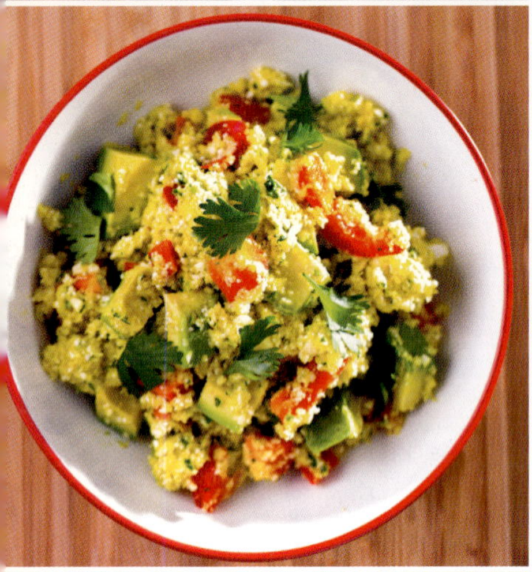
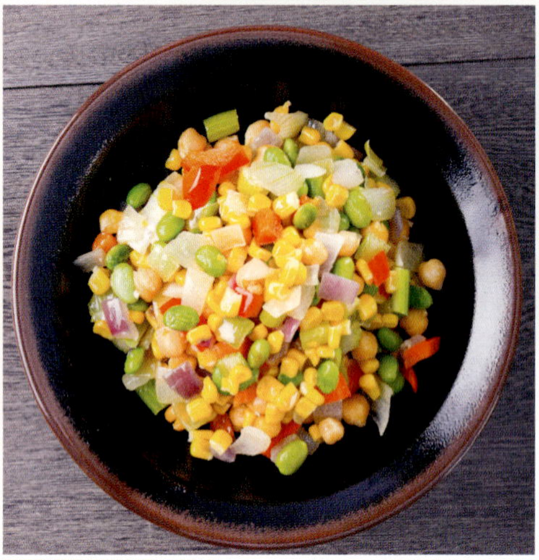
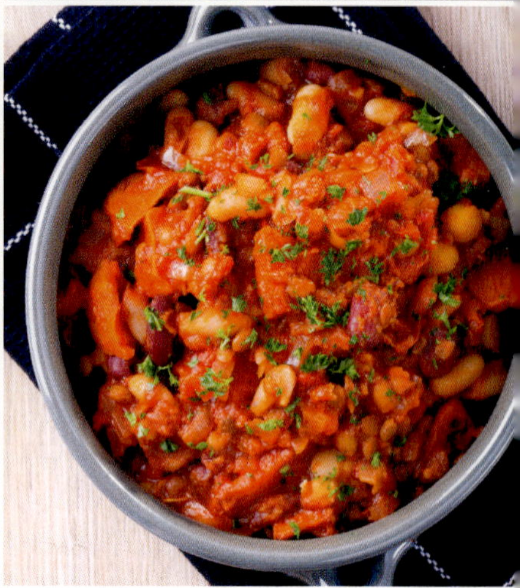
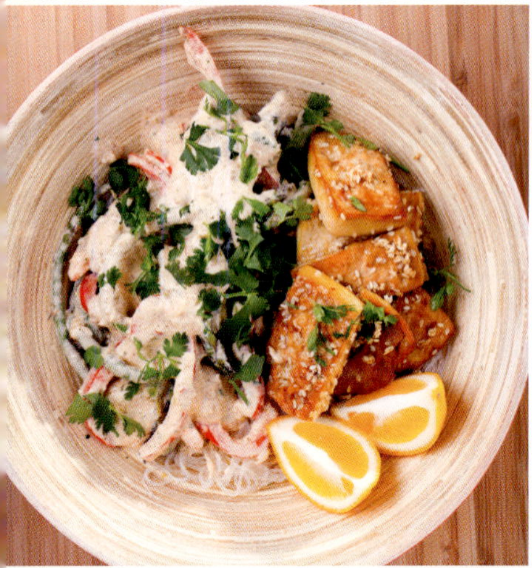
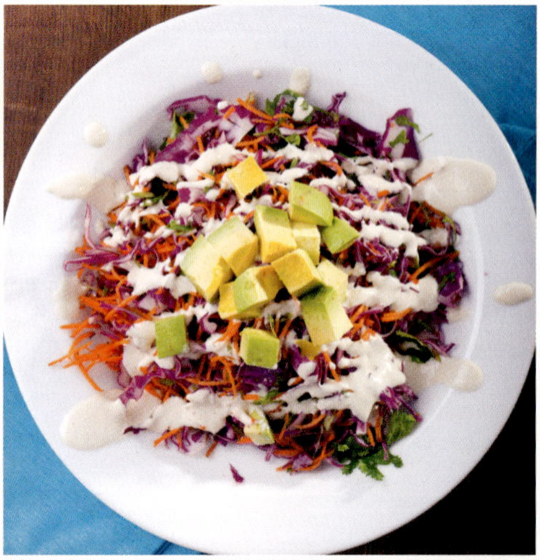
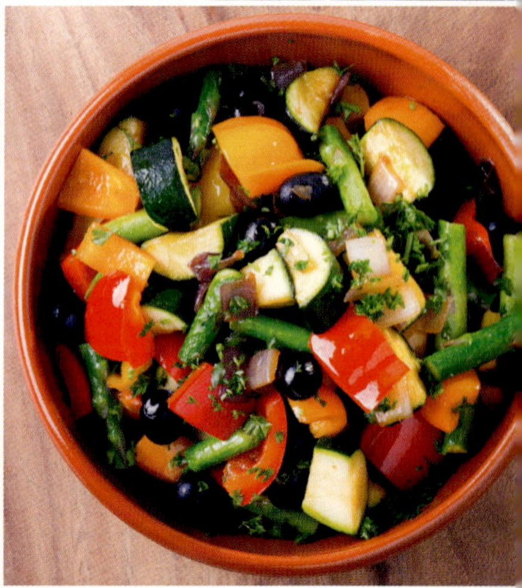
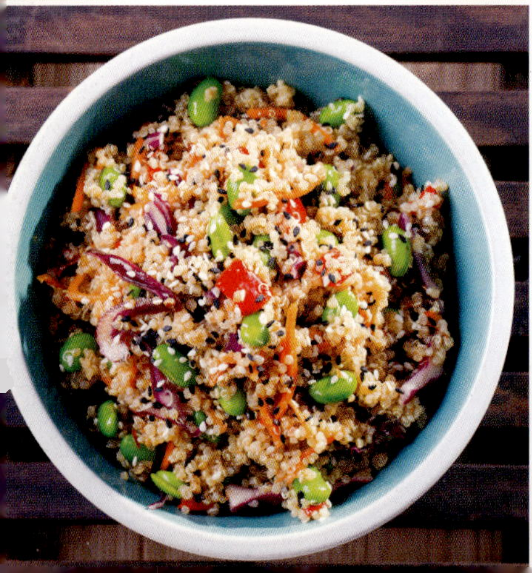
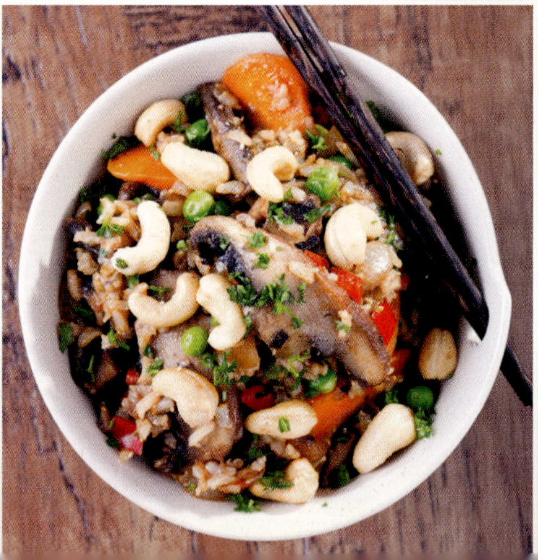
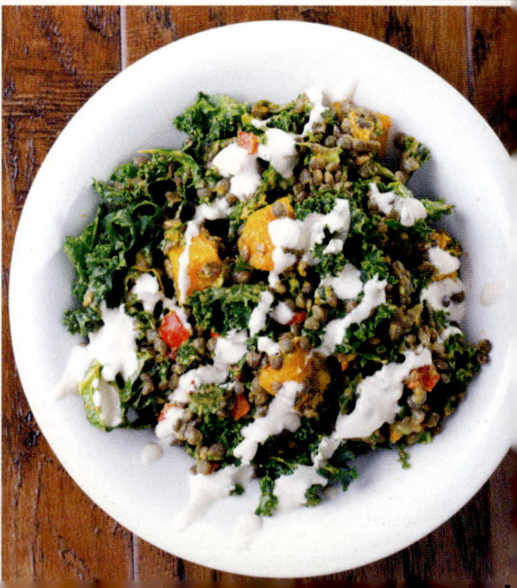

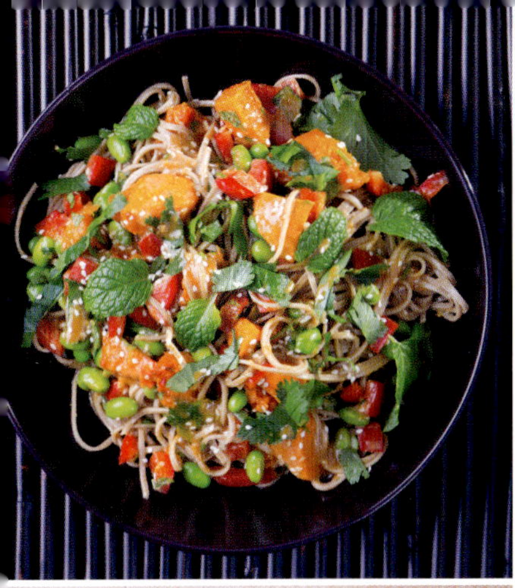
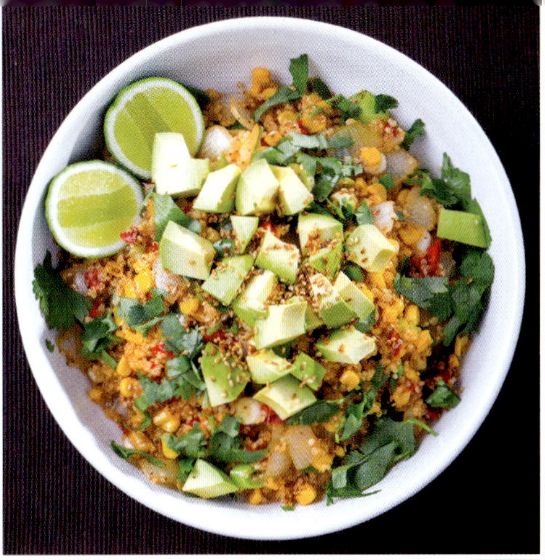
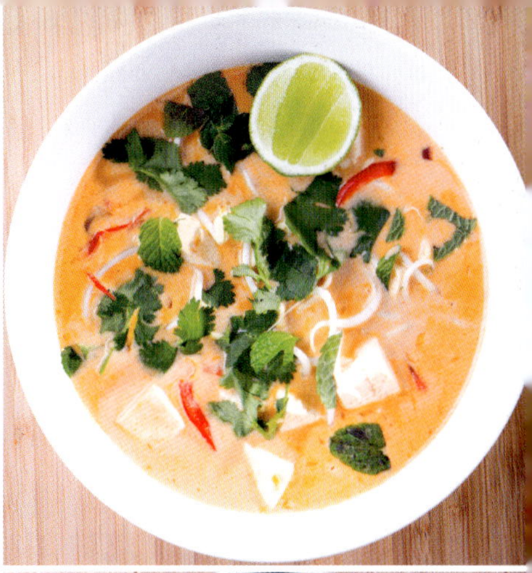
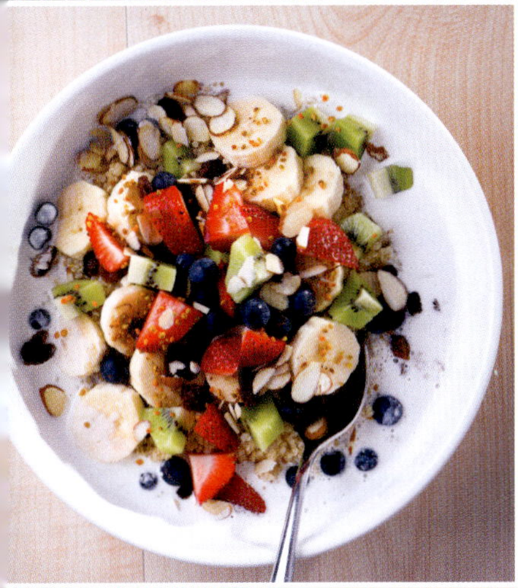
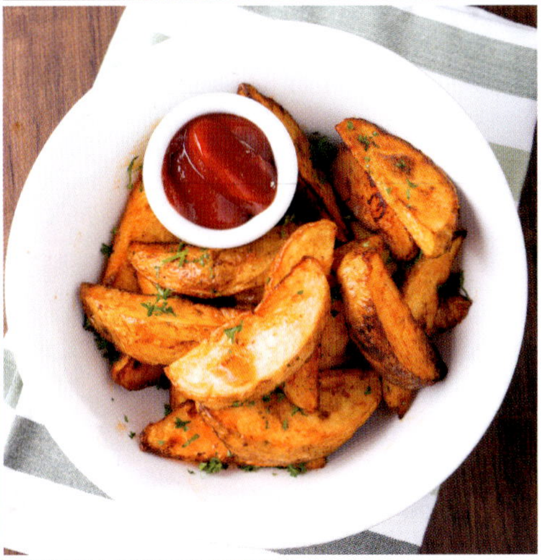
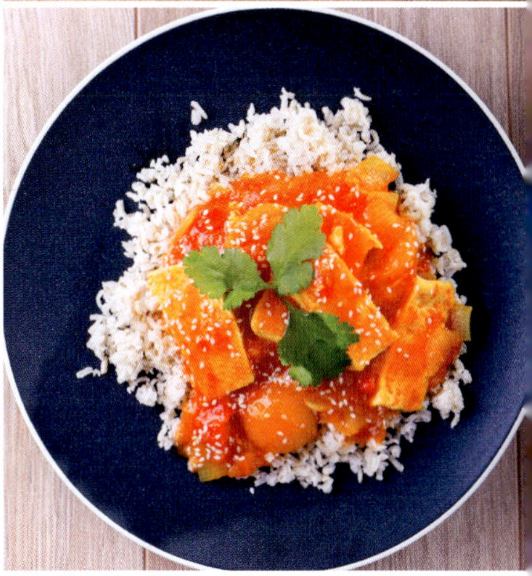
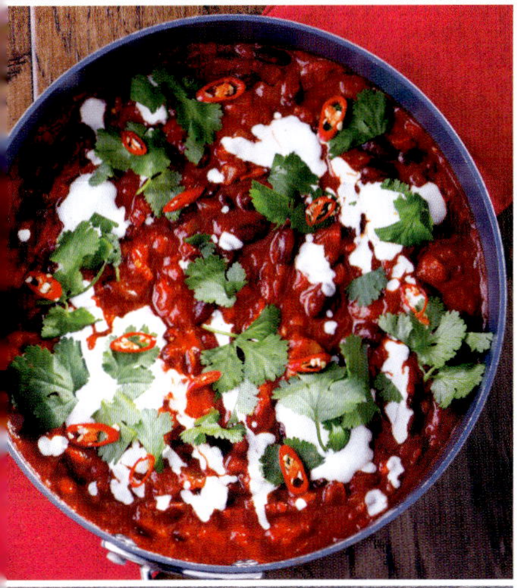
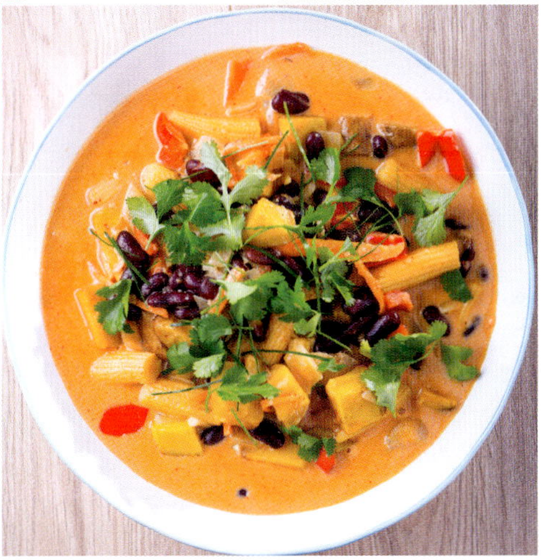
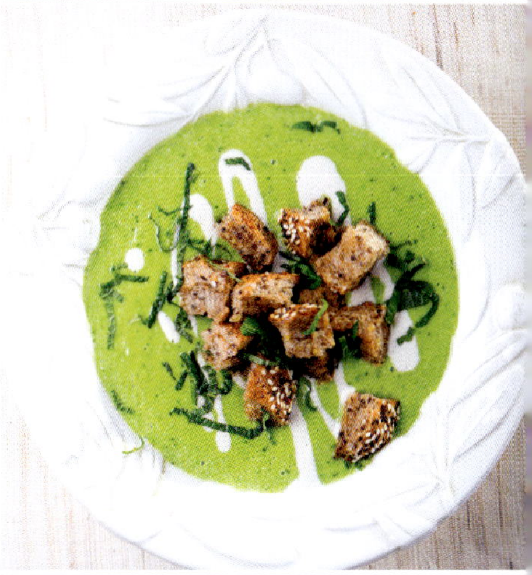
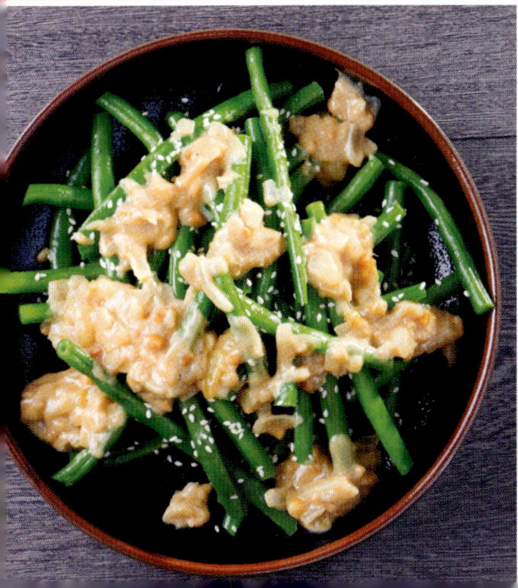
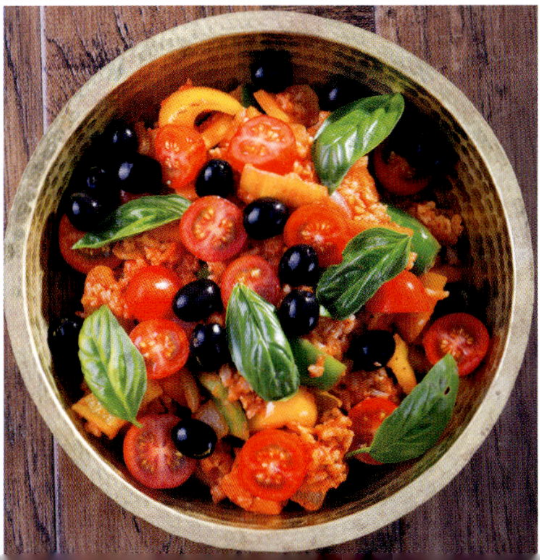
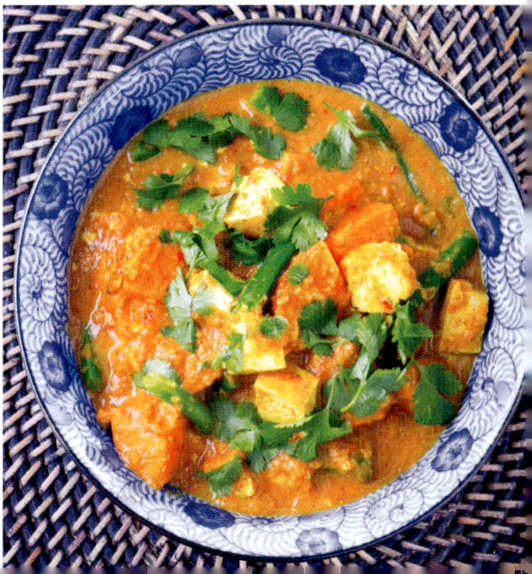

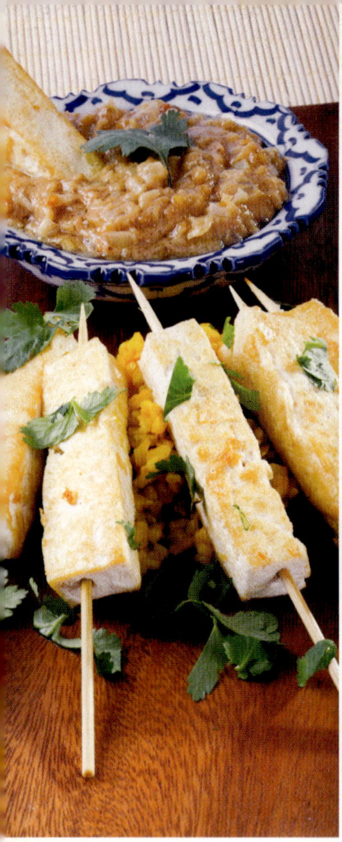
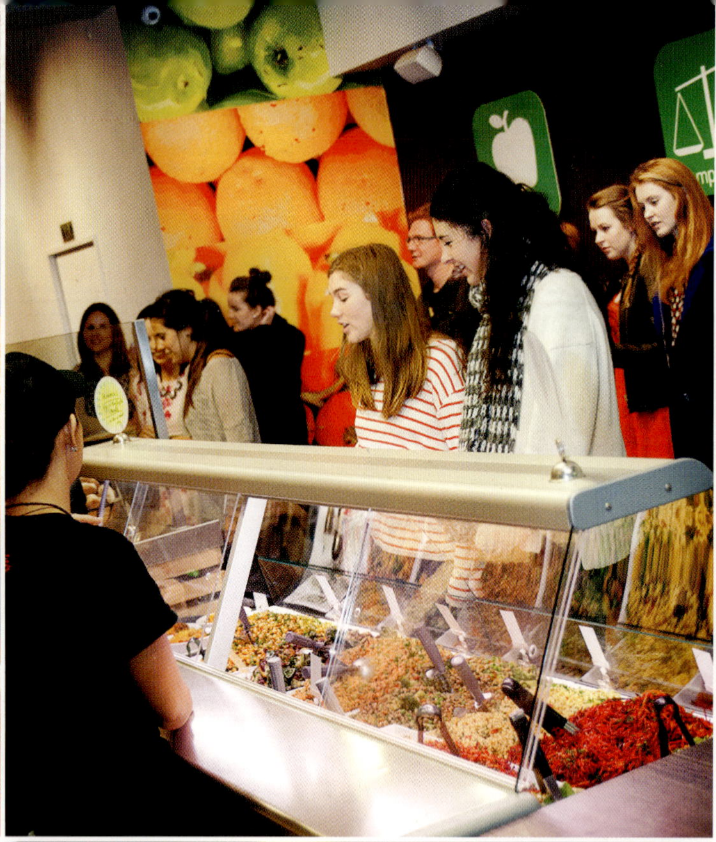
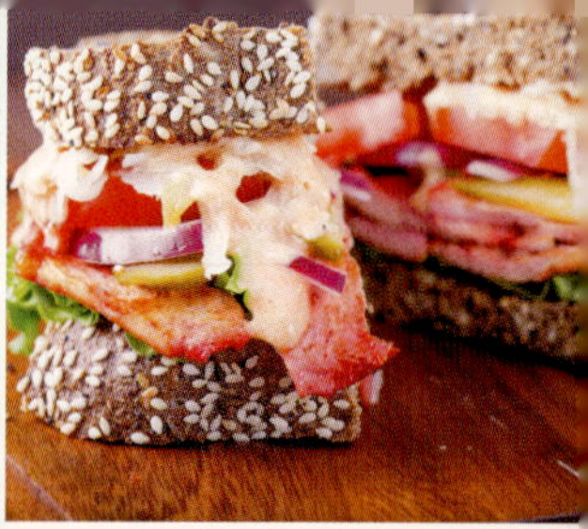
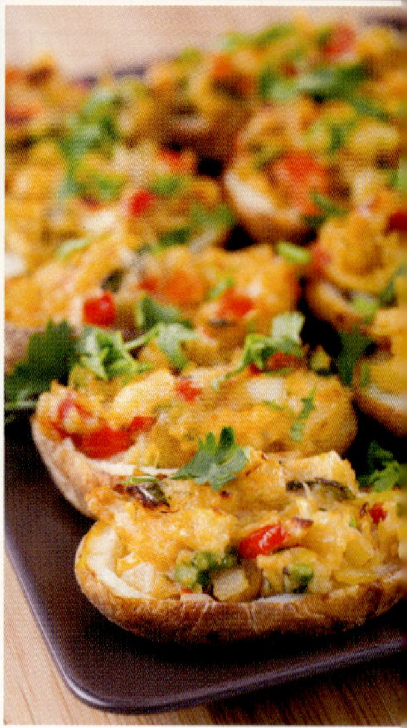
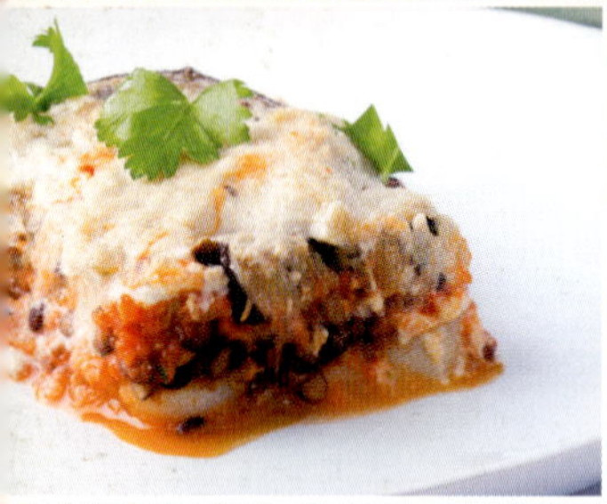
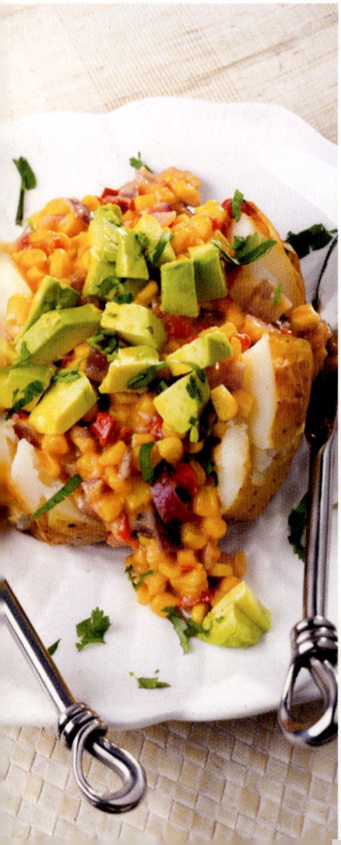
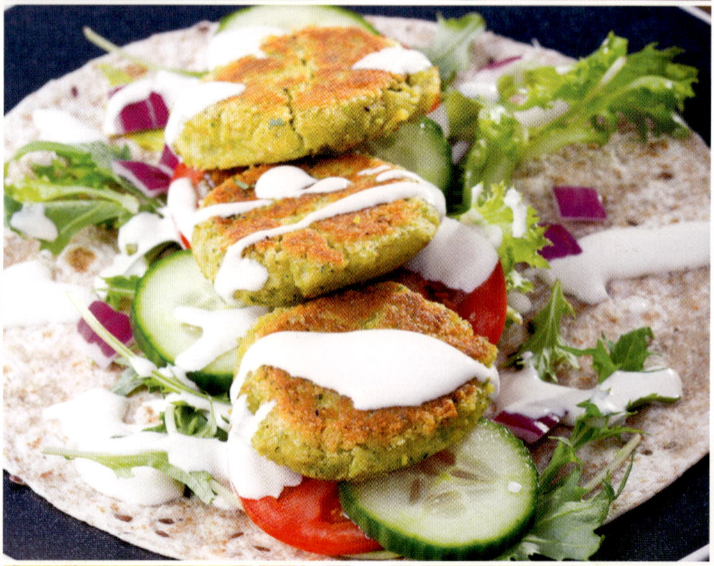
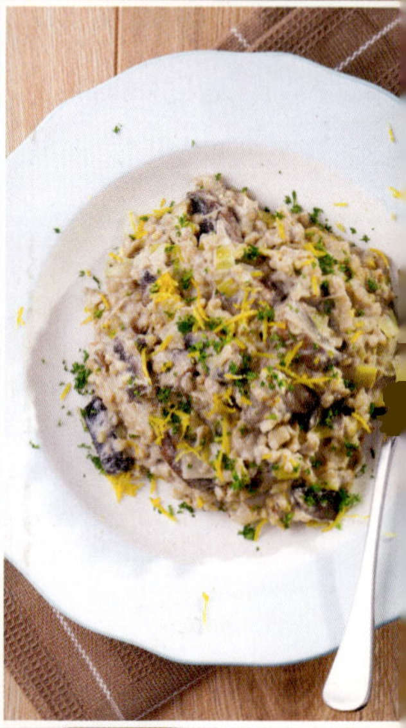
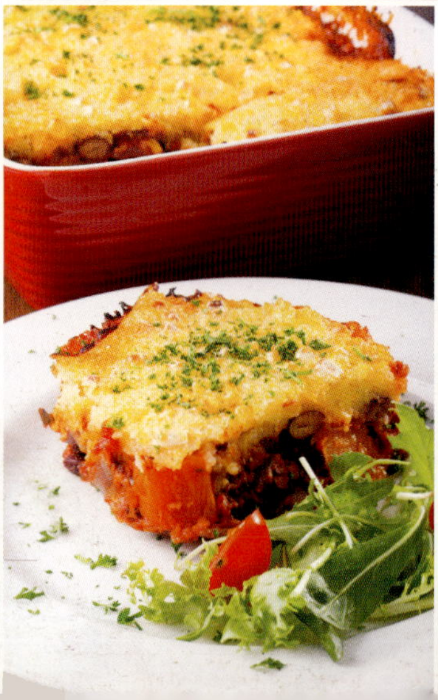
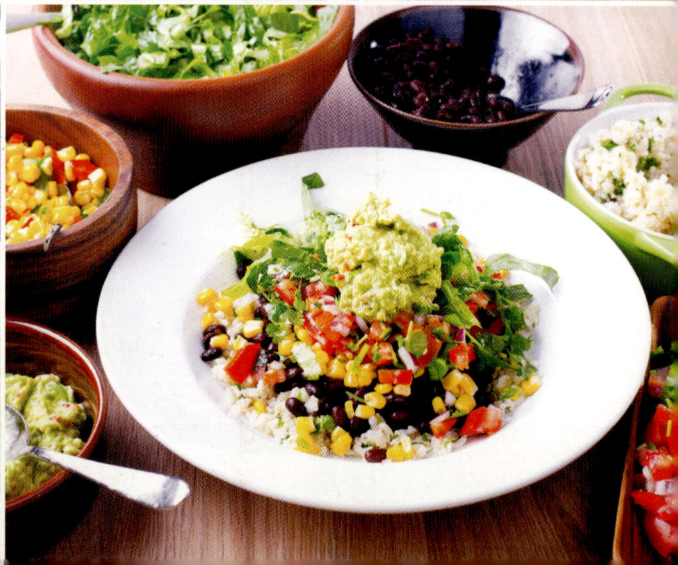

Main Meals

Falafel Pita Wraps 82

Creamed Corn Baked Potato 84

Turkish Moussaka 86

Energising Mexican Feast 88

Satay Tofu Kebabs 90

Tamale Pie 92

Thai Infused Baked Potatoes 94

Reuben Burger 96

Mushroom & Leek Buckwheat Risotto 98

I used to get the falafel mixes from the supermarket, and these are great. Verity, my wife, suggested that I try making my own from scratch. I was hesitant at first as all the ingredients on the pre-made versions made it look complicated. But after 2 attempts with a much simpler ingredient list, I had the perfect recipe nailed.

Falafel Pita Wraps

MAKES 24

FALAFEL:

- 1 cup chickpeas dried
- 2 cups edamame (green soy beans) or broad beans (fava beans)
- 1 teaspoon salt
- 1 cup coriander (cilantro) roughly chopped
- 1 teaspoon cumin powder
- 1 medium onion quartered
- 2 cloves garlic
- ½ cup chickpea (besan/chana) flour
- oil for shallow frying

WRAPS:

- 4 wholemeal wraps
- tomato
- cucumber
- mesclun (or other) lettuce
- chopped red onion
- Tahini Dressing (page 171)
- optional: diced avocado

1. Soak the dried chickpeas in at least 3 cups of water for 5 hours or more. These will nearly triple in size.

2. If using the frozen beans or chickpeas, soak them in hot water for 30 seconds to defrost them.

3. Put all the falafel ingredients into a food processor and process until a consistent mix.

4. Spoon out 2 tablespoon balls and flatten.

5. Shallow fry in a non-stick frying pan with a little oil. Around 2 minutes per side or until golden.

6. Serve with salad vegetables on wholemeal pita bread. Wrap up and eat!

This recipe calls for chickpeas that are soaked (not cooked). You can use cooked chickpeas if you like, however you will get a smoother (and less authentic) mixture and you will need to add an extra cup of chickpea flour.

You can find edamame or broad beans in the freezer at whole-food or Asian grocery stores.

Wholemeal Wraps

It is sometimes nice having a wrap instead of a sandwich. You may have to hunt for wholemeal varieties but they are out there. Just add some form of protein, some fresh vegetables and a dressing and you have a great meal. Wraps are also great for making burritos too.

MAIN MEALS 83

I love baked potatoes and it is a great "feed a crowd" choice. Often when we have friends around I will bake up a whole lot of potatoes and make a handful of delicious toppings. You may have used normal creamed corn out of the tin for baked potatoes, however a few minutes creating your own mixture will transform your baked potato!

Creamed Corn Baked Potato

MAKES 4 SERVES

- 4 large potatoes
- 1½ cups red onion diced (around 1 onion)
- 1 cup red capsicum (bell pepper) diced (around 1 capsicum)
- 2 cloves garlic finely chopped or crushed
- 1 teaspoon oil
- 2 cups frozen corn (or tinned)
- 1 tablespoon honey or date puree
- ½ teaspoon salt
- 2 tablespoons arrowroot
- ½ cup cashew nuts raw (or almonds raw)
- 1 cup water
- 1 avocado diced
- garnish: fresh coriander (cilantro)

1. Put the potatoes in the oven and bake at 180°C (350°F) for around 1 hour or until soft in the middle.

2. In a pot or pan, saute the onion, capsicum, garlic and oil for around 5 minutes or until soft.

3. Add the corn, honey and salt.

4. In a blender, blend the arrowroot, cashews and water until smooth. Pour in to the corn mixture and stir until it thickens up.

5. Cut the potato on top with a cross shape and squeeze the sides to open the top like a flower.

6. Cover with the creamed corn, avocado and coriander.

Baked Potatoes

These form the basis of a great meal. You just need to be organised and plan ahead of time. I will often put the potatoes in the oven in the morning and set the timer so they are finished cooking just before I get home. There is nothing like coming home to a kitchen smelling of baked potatoes.

MAIN MEALS 85

This is a classic meal we serve at Revive. The prep required is a little more work than other recipes but it is worth it!

Turkish Moussaka

MAKES 8 SERVES

4 cups Italian Tomato Sauce (page 174)

6 cups potato sliced thinly (around 2 medium potatoes)

1 large eggplant (aubergine) sliced thickly (around 12 large slices)

1 tablespoon oil

¼ teaspoon salt

400g (12oz) tin brown lentils

CASHEW SAUCE:

1 cup cashew nuts raw

2¼ cups water

½ teaspoon salt

3 tablespoons nutritional flaked yeast

½ teaspoon arrowroot

garnish: Italian parsley or fresh coriander (cilantro)

1. Make the Italian Tomato Sauce.
2. Put the potato in a pot of boiling water and cook for around 10 minutes or until it is getting soft and starting to break apart.
3. Mix the eggplant, oil, and salt together and put on an oven tray. Bake at 180°C (350°F) for around 10 minutes or until it starts getting soft.
4. Put the cashew sauce ingredients into a blender and blend until smooth. Cook in a pot while stirring for a couple of minutes until it thickens up.
5. In a 25x20cm (10x8in) rectangular dish, layer the ingredients: Half the tomato sauce on the bottom, followed by the potato, followed by the lentils, followed by the remaining tomato sauce.
6. Distribute the eggplant and pour over the cashew sauce.
7. Bake at 180°C (350°F) for around 30 minutes or until it is cooked through.
8. Serve with a garnish of Italian parsley or coriander.

You can serve immediately, or let it sit for half an hour and it will firm up.

You can use a healthy jar of tomato sauce if you do not have time to make the Italian Tomato Sauce.

MAIN MEALS 87

Some Mexican fast food chains offer a "naked burrito" which is all the burrito ingredients without the burrito. This is a great way to have a Mexican meal for the family. Most chains will include sour cream and meat, however these wholesome plant-based ingredients are all you need!

Energising Mexican Feast

MAKES 6 X 2 CUP SERVES

2 cups Tangy Coriander Rice (page 134)

2½ cups Mexican Salsa (page 164)

400g (12oz) tin black beans

3 cups cos (romaine) lettuce sliced

400g (12oz) tin whole kernel corn (drained)

1 cup Avocado Guacamole (page 177)

1. Make the rice and tomato salsa.

2. Heat the beans in a pot on the stove.

3. Prepare the vegetables and guacamole.

4. Put all of the ingredients in bowls around the table and let everyone customise their own Mexican feast!

5. Generally start with the rice and beans. Then layer the other ingredients finishing with the guacamole on top.

For even more flavour, you can substitute the regular corn kernels with my Corn & Pepper Fiesta recipe from The Revive Cafe Cookbook 1 (page 48).

MAIN MEALS 89

Satay Tofu Kebabs

Anything with satay sauce is very very yummy. It is a great match with tofu which has a very neutral flavour.

MAKES 12 SERVES

KEBABS:

600g (18oz) block firm tofu cut into strips

2 tablespoons oil

1 teaspoon salt

12 bamboo skewers

SPICY SATAY SAUCE:

1 cup onions

1 tablespoon ginger puree or finely chopped

4 cloves garlic finely chopped or crushed

1 tablespoon oil

optional: 1 chilli de-seeded and finely diced

1 teaspoon cumin

1 teaspoon coriander

6 tablespoons peanut butter

½ cup hot water

1 tablespoon honey or date puree

serve with: cooked brown rice with turmeric

garnish: fresh coriander (cilantro) chopped

1. Push the skewers through the tofu strips. In a non-stick pan saute the tofu and oil for around 10 minutes until they are golden brown. Sprinkle with salt.

2. In a pot or pan saute the onions, ginger, garlic and oil until the onions are clear. Stir in the optional chilli, cumin and coriander.

3. In a cup mix the peanut butter with the water so it is a runny paste.

4. Add the peanut paste and honey to the onion mix. Bring back to the heat while stirring.

5. You may need to add a little more water to adjust the consistency. However only add small amounts as it does not take much to turn it from a nice thick satay into a runny one.

6. Serve the kebabs on brown rice which has a little tumeric added to make it yellow. Drizzle over the satay sauce and garnish with some coriander.

If your skewers are too long just trim them carefully on the blunt end with a sharp knife.

Bamboo Skewers

Available from most supermarkets, these are great for tofu kebabs, vegetable kebabs, fruit kebabs. They are also useful for holding together un-cooperative burgers.

MAIN MEALS 91

Tamale Pie

One of my friends and recipe testers, Nyree, asked me to make a healthy version of this pie. It is so simple to make. The trick is getting the right consistency with the base (so it is not dry or too watery). The corn topping in most Tamale Pie recipes comes with cheese, however this one still tastes great without it!

MAKES 8 LARGE SERVES

CORN TOPPING

- 1 cup coarse polenta (cornmeal)
- 3 cups cold water
- ¾ teaspoon salt
- 3 cups frozen corn (or tinned)

BASE

- 2 cups pumpkin or butternut squashed chopped into 2cm (1in) cubes
- 2 teaspoons oil
- 1 cup red onion diced (around 1 small onion)
- 1 cup onion diced (around 1 small onion)
- 3 cloves garlic finely chopped or crushed
- 1 tablespoon oil
- 2 cups chopped courgettes (zucchini) (around 2 medium)
- 1 cup red capsicum (bell pepper) roughly diced (around 1)
- 1 tablespoon honey or date puree
- 400g (12oz) tin chopped tomatoes
- 400g (12oz) tin red kidney beans (drained)
- ¾ teaspoon salt
- 4 tablespoons tomato paste
- 1 teaspoon mixed herbs

1. In a pot combine the polenta, water and salt and bring to the boil stirring regularly. Add the frozen corn and stir in.

2. In a bowl mix the pumpkin and oil together. Put onto an oven tray and bake at 180°C (350°F) for around 15 minutes or until just getting soft.

3. In another pot saute the onion, garlic and oil for around 5 minutes or until clear. Add the courgettes and capsicum and saute for another couple of minutes until they are slightly soft.

4. Add the honey, tomatoes, kidney beans, salt, tomato paste, mixed herbs and roasted pumpkin and heat until it is just bubbling.

5. Pour the vegetable mixture into a baking dish approx. 20x30cm (8x12in). Spoon the corn topping on top and spread around evenly.

6. Bake at 180°C (350°F) for around 30 minutes or until the topping is firm.

It will be easier to serve if you let it sit and cool for around 30 minutes to firm up if you have time.

Polenta (Cornmeal)

This grain is made from finely ground corn. It can be used for pizza bases or as toppings like this recipe. It is also useful as a "dusting" for patties and other similar meals.

MAIN MEALS 93

These yummy potatoes are amazing. They are also great as finger food if you can find some really small potatoes (and have the time).

Thai Infused Baked Potatoes

MAKES 24

12 small potatoes

1½ cups onion finely sliced (around 1 large onion)

1 teaspoon oil

2 tablespoons finely chopped fresh or frozen lemongrass

2 cloves garlic finely chopped or crushed

1 cup cashew nuts raw

1 cup red capsicum (bell pepper) finely diced (around 1 capsicum)

2 cups fresh asparagus (ends broken off) cut into small cubes

1 teaspoon Thai red curry paste

½ cup hot water

1 tablespoon honey

1 teaspoon salt

½ cup soy milk or milk of your choice

oil for brushing/spraying

garnish: fresh coriander (cilantro)

1. Roast the potatoes in the oven at 180°C (350°F) for 1 hour or until soft. Leave to cool slightly. Scoop out the potato into a bowl leaving a shell.

2. In a pot saute the onion, lemongrass, garlic and oil for 5 minutes or until the onion is soft.

3. Add the cashew nuts, capsicum and asparagus and cook for another 5 minutes or until the capsicum is soft.

4. Mix the curry paste with the hot water and mix into the pot.

5. Add the honey, salt and milk and mix into the pot.

6. Stir the potato into the pot and mash around.

7. Spoon the potato and vegetable mixture into the potato shells.

8. Lightly brush or spray the tops with some oil.

9. Grill (broil) for around 5 minutes or until the tops start to brown.

10. Garnish with fresh coriander.

MAIN MEALS 95

This is a popular burger found everywhere in North America. It is made special by using a southwestern dressing and sauerkraut (fermented cabbage). It is a tangy burger and all the flavours work together for a taste sensation! Here is my healthy version.

Reuben Burger

MAKES 2 LARGE BURGERS

4 slices of wholemeal bread or 2 wholemeal burger buns

TOFU:

300g (10oz) firm tofu sliced thinly

1 teaspoon oil

½ medium beetroot grated (retaining juice)

¼ teaspoon salt

DRESSING:

4 tablespoons Revive Aioli (page 174)

1 tablespoon ketchup

FILLINGS:

1 large tomato sliced

4 tablespoons sauerkraut (fermented cabbage)

¼ red onion sliced into rings

2 gherkins (pickles) sliced

lettuce

1. In a non-stick pan, saute the tofu and oil for around 5 minutes or until starting to brown.

2. Take the grated beetroot and squeeze above the tofu so it becomes a pink colour. Sprinkle the salt on the tofu.

3. Mix the ketchup with the aioli to make the southwestern dressing.

4. Layer the bread with the tofu, fillings and dressing.

Sauerkraut

This is fermented cabbage with a tangy sour flavour. It is a very tasty addition to this burger. Fermented foods can be really good for your digestive system.

MAIN MEALS 97

I was originally going to do this dish with rice or Israeli couscous (which it would work well with). However I saw some lonely buckwheat on my pantry shelf needing some love. Buckwheat has a very raw taste when cooked and you need to mask it with strong flavours. I thought this dish did not succeed then at the end I added the lemon juice and it just transformed it. So make sure you do not leave out this ingredient!

Mushroom & Leek Buckwheat Risotto

MAKES 5 X 1 CUP SERVES

- ¾ cup buckwheat
- 1½ cups boiling water
- 3 cloves garlic finely chopped or crushed
- 2 cups leeks sliced (around 1 large leek)
- 250g (8oz) flat mushrooms (around 4 large mushrooms) halved and sliced
- 1 tablespoon oil
- 1 cup cashew nuts raw
- 1½ cups water
- 1 teaspoon salt
- 1 tablespoon soy sauce
- 4 tablespoons lemon juice (around 2 lemons)
- garnish: lemon zest
- garnish parsley

1. In a pot combine the buckwheat and boiling water and heat to bring back to the boil. Turn down to low and simmer with the lid on for 15 minutes or until the water has gone and the buckwheat is soft. This should yield 2 cups of cooked buckwheat.

2. In a pot or pan saute the garlic, leeks, mushrooms and oil for around 10 minutes or until everything is soft. Add the cooked buckwheat.

3. In a blender, blend the cashews and water until smooth. Add to the risotto.

4. Add the salt and soy sauce and heat until bubbling while stirring.

5. Grate the zest of the lemons using the fine grater side on your box grater. Do this before you squeeze the lemon juice.

6. Before serving stir in the lemon juice.

7. Serve garnished with parsley and lemon zest.

This is also excellent with 2 cups of frozen peas added at step 4.

Lemon Zest

You will usually throw away your lemon skins, so this is essentially a free ingredient! Grate with a special lemon zester or just use the fine grating side of your box grater. Make sure you only grate the yellow part and not the white pith.

MAIN MEALS | 99

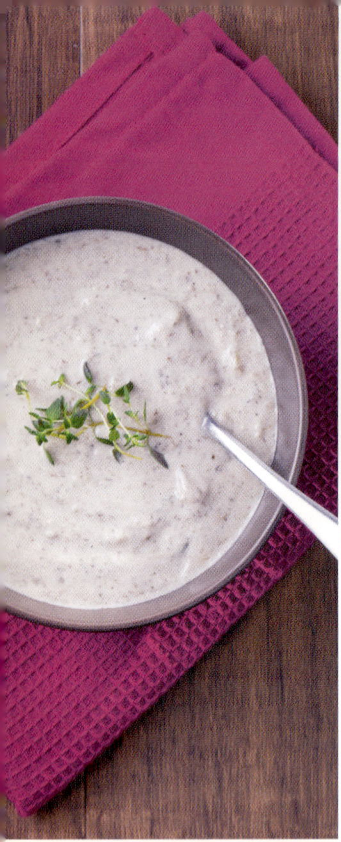
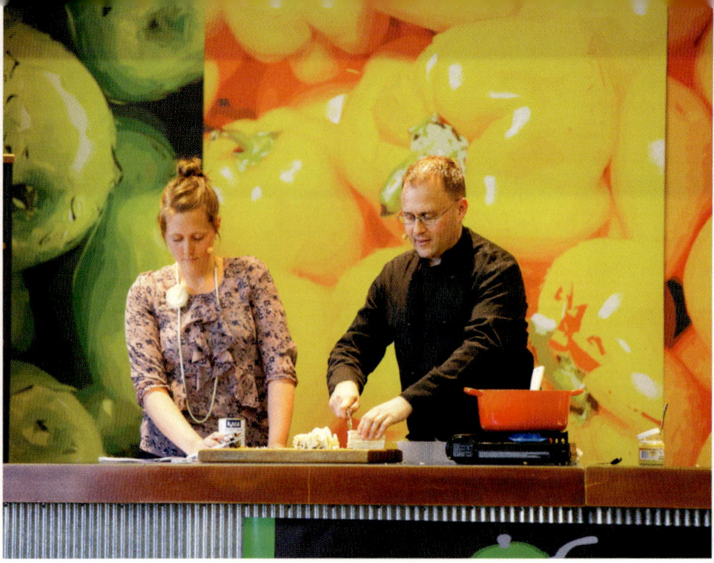
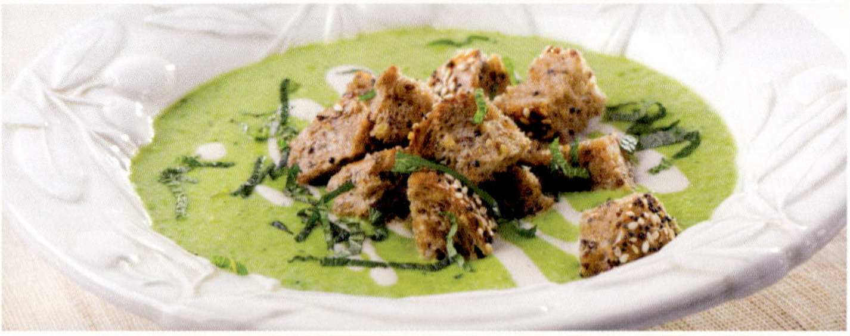
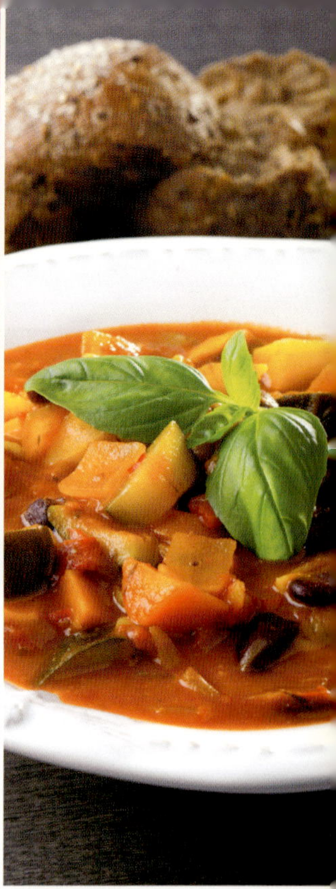
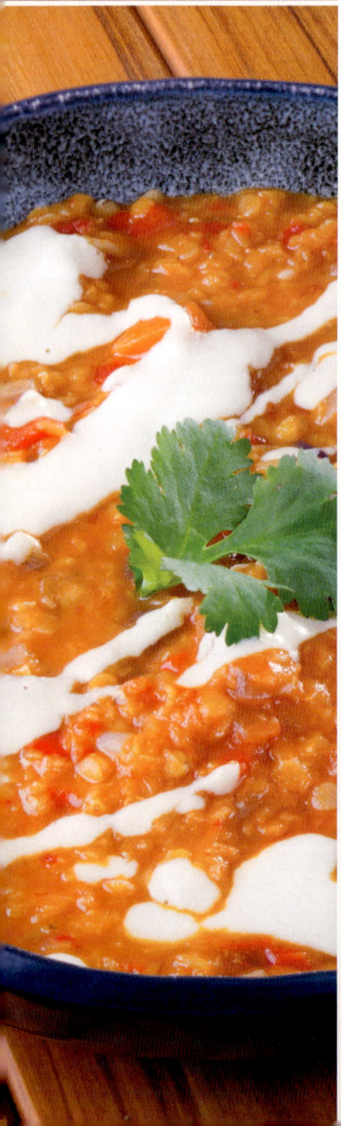
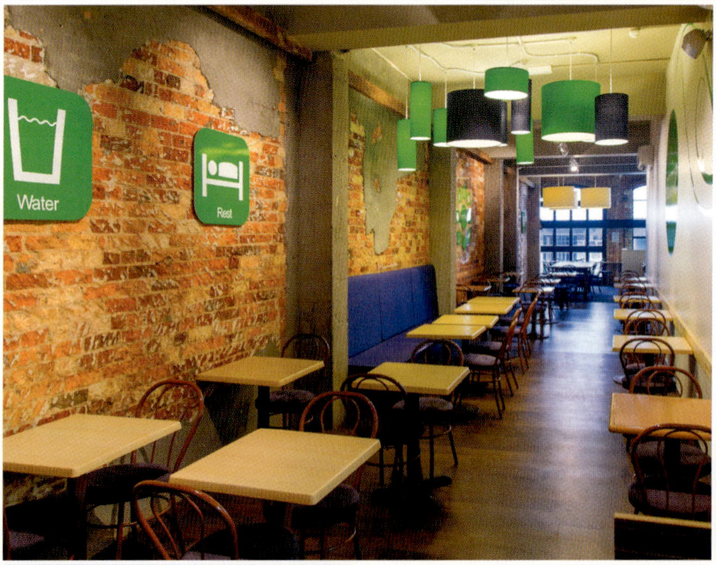
Water
Rest
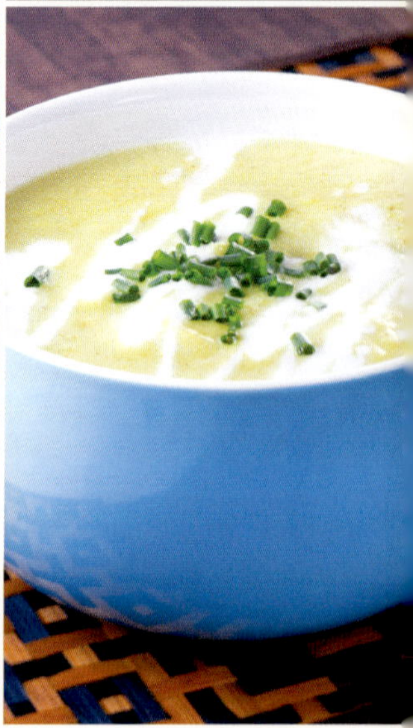
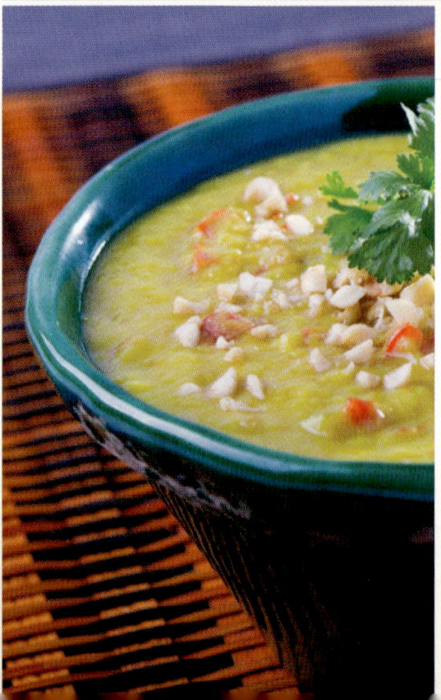
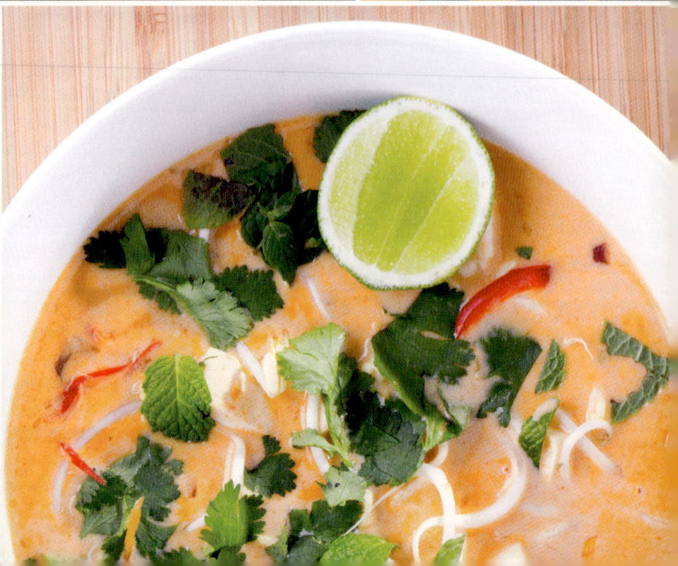

Soups

Chunky Vegetable & Lentil Soup 102

Creamy & Minty Pea Soup 104

Mushroom & Thyme Soup 106

Satay Sweet Potato Bisque 108

Minestrone 110

Malaysian Laksa 112

Curried Cauliflower Soup 114

My wife Verity loves lentils. Whenever I give her some options I want to make for dinner she usually asks "... and with lentils?". This soup was originally going to be just a vegetable soup but became a lentil soup as well! And tastes amazing. The best part about red lentils is they cook very quickly and are inexpensive, so make sure you have a good supply in your pantry.

Chunky Vegetable & Lentil Soup

MAKES 9 X 1 CUP SERVES

1 tablespoon oil

2 cups red onion diced (around 1 large)

4 cloves garlic finely chopped or crushed

1 tablespoon finely chopped ginger or ginger puree

2 cups carrot diced (around 3 medium carrots)

2 cups red capsicum (bell pepper) finely diced (around 2 capsicum)

1½ cups red lentils

6 cups boiling water

¼ cup tomato paste

1 teaspoon salt

garnish: Classic Hummus (page 177)

1. In a large pot or pan, saute the oil, onion, garlic, ginger, carrot and capsicum until all is very soft.

2. Add the lentils and water and simmer for around 15 minutes or with lentils are soft.

3. Stir in the tomato paste and salt.

4. Serve with some hummus on top.

Hummus is best with soups like this in a runny form. Just take normal hummus and stir some water into it.

If you prefer a creamier and smooth soup just whip out your stick blender and blend part or all of the soup.

SOUPS 103

I had heard of pea soups but thought they would taste average. I thought I would try one with a few healthy tweaks without using cream. I tried it and it was amazing - way beyond my expectations. The wholemeal croutons are great too!

Creamy & Minty Pea Soup

MAKES 5 x 1 CUP SERVES

CROUTONS:

2 wholemeal buns or 4 slices wholemeal bread

1 teaspoon oil

¼ teaspoon salt

SOUP:

1 cup onion roughly chopped (around 1 onion)

3 cloves garlic finely chopped or crushed

2 teaspoons oil

3 cups frozen peas

4 cups boiling water

¾ cup cashew nuts raw

1 cup hot water

1 teaspoon salt

¼ cup fresh mint

garnish: mint

1. Cut the bread into 1cm (½in) cubes. Mix with the oil and salt in a bowl.

2. Put on to a baking tray and bake at 150°C (300°F) for around 5 minutes or until crispy on the outside (but not hard all the way through).

3. In a pot saute the onion, garlic and oil for around 5 minutes or until the onion is soft.

4. Add the frozen peas and boiling water and cook for 5 minutes or until the peas are just cooked. Do not overcook.

5. In a blender, blend the cashews and hot water until smooth. Add to the soup and reserve a little for garnish.

6. Add the salt and mint and blend the soup with a stick blender until smooth.

7. Serve with a garnish of mint, cashew cream and the warm croutons on top.

When purchasing peas, be aware that most minted peas only contain "mint flavouring" not actual mint.

Croutons

These little guys can transform a soup. Just roast some wholemeal bread with a little salt and oil. Best when warm. Just avoid the pre-processed preservative infused supermarket white bread croutons - they are not really fit for human consumption.

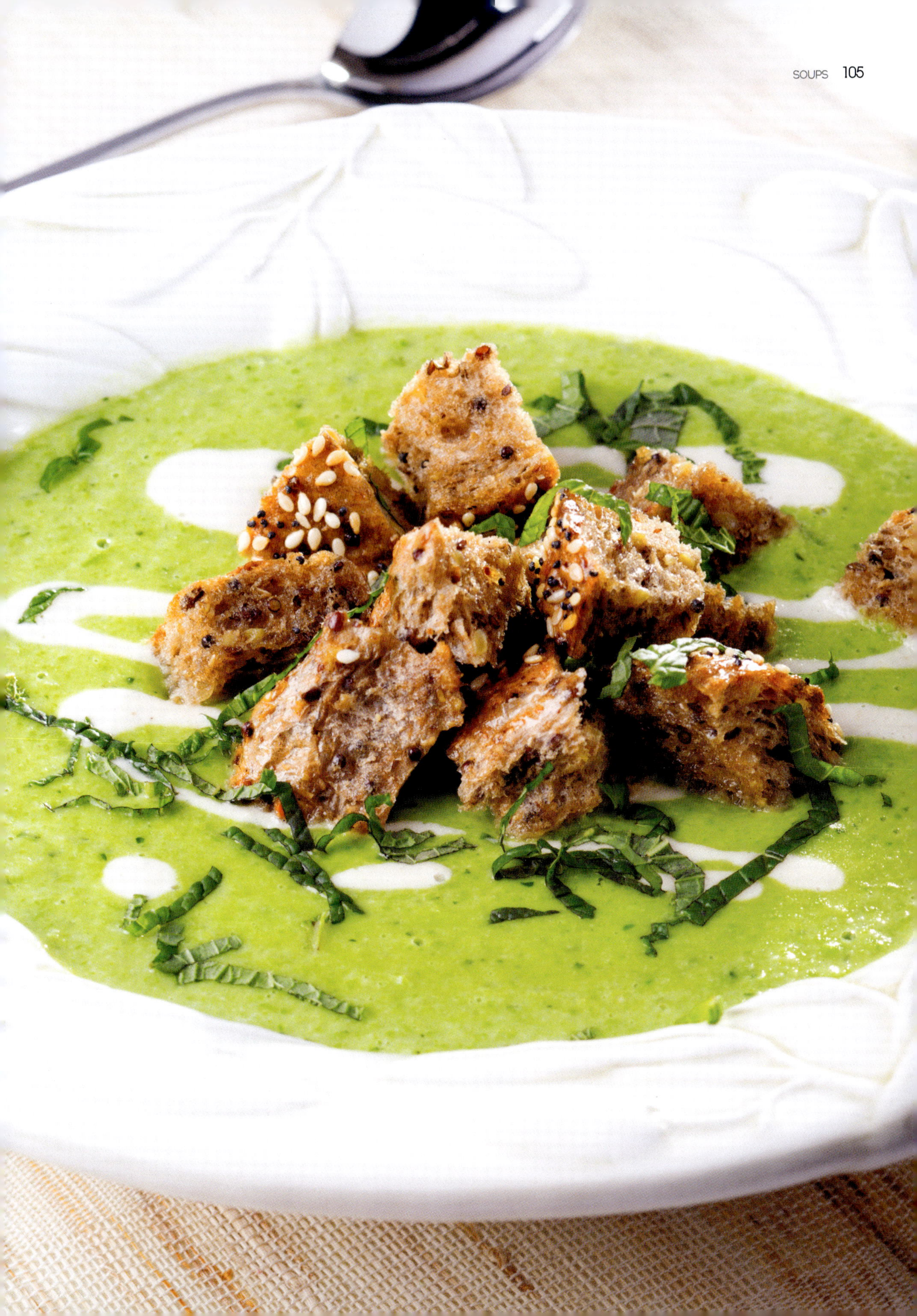

I love mushrooms whole and have usually balked at any request to make mushroom soup as it is a waste of whole mushrooms. But every cookbook series needs a mushroom soup so I succumbed to the pressure. And I love it! Most mushroom soups are loaded with cream so this version uses cashew cream instead.

Mushroom & Thyme Soup

MAKES 5 X 1 CUP SERVES

1½ cups onions diced (around 1 large onion)

250g (8oz) flat mushrooms (around 4 large mushrooms) roughly sliced

4 cloves garlic crushed or finely chopped

2 teaspoons dried thyme (or fresh if you have it)

1 tablespoon oil

¾ cup cashew nuts raw

2 cups water

1 teaspoon salt

garnish: fresh thyme

1. In a pot saute the onions, mushrooms, garlic, thyme and oil for around 5 minutes or until the onions are soft.

2. In a blender, blend the cashew nuts and water.

3. Add to the mushroom mix and add the salt and heat the soup until it is just bubbling.

4. With a stick blender, blend the mixture so it is smooth.

5. Serve garnished with fresh thyme.

You could use any kind of mushrooms for this dish.

Fresh Thyme

Thyme goes well with mushrooms. It is easy to grow in your garden too. The best way to get the leaves off is to hold the leaf at the top and run your finger down to the base, which will pull off the leaves.

SOUPS 107

Sweet potatoes make awesome soups. This one combines them with satay peanut flavours! You can also use other nuts or nut butters like cashew or almond if you do not like peanuts.

Satay Sweet Potato Bisque

MAKES 10 X 1 CUP SERVES

1½ cups onions diced (around 1 large onion)

1 cup celery cubed (around 2 stalks)

1 teaspoon oil

1 tablespoon finely chopped ginger or ginger puree

4 cloves garlic crushed or finely chopped

1 teaspoon salt

1 teaspoon turmeric

1 teaspoon cumin

6 cups red kumara (sweet potato) chopped (around 3 large kumara)

5 cups boiling water

½ cup peanut butter mixed with ½ cup hot water

1 cup red capsicum (bell pepper) finely diced (around 1 capsicum)

garnish: chopped peanuts

garnish: coriander (cilantro)

1. In a pot saute the onion, celery, oil, ginger and garlic for around 5 minutes or until the onion is soft.

2. Add the salt and spices and mix around for around 30 seconds.

3. Add the kumara and water, bring back to the boil, and simmer for around 15 minutes or until the kumara is soft.

4. Add the peanut butter and hot water mix and the red capsicum.

5. Serve garnished with some chopped peanuts and coriander.

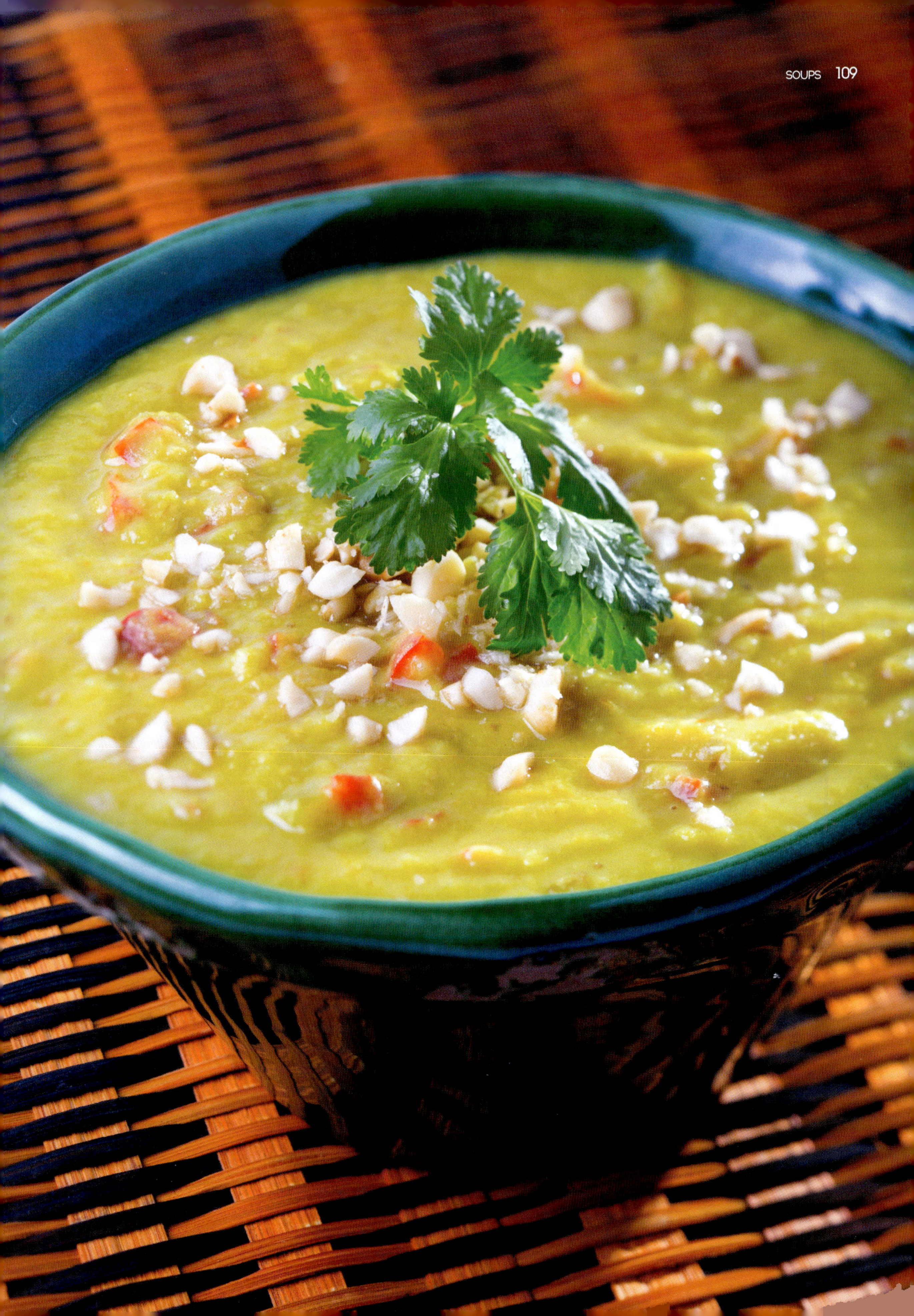

Minestrone

A lovely warming winter soup.

MAKES 16 X 1 CUP SERVES

1 tablespoon oil

4 cloves garlic crushed or finely chopped

1½ cups onion diced chunky (around 1 onion)

1½ cups celery sliced 1cm (around 2 stalks)

8 cups boiling water

2 x 400g (12oz) cans crushed tomatoes

1½ cups carrots diced 1cm (½in) (around 1 large)

1 cup potato diced 1cm (½in) (around 1 medium)

1½ cup leeks sliced (around 1 medium leek)

1½ cups courgettes (zucchini) (1 large)

1 tablespoon dried mixed herbs

2 cups wholemeal shell pasta (or shape of your choice)

400g (12oz) tin red kidney beans (drained)

1 teaspoon salt

2 tablespoons honey

garnish: fresh basil

1. In a pot saute the oil, garlic, onion, celery until the onion is soft.

2. Add the water, tomatoes, rest of the vegetables and mixed herbs. Bring to the boil and turn down and simmer for around 15 minutes.

3. Add the pasta and cook for another 5-10 minutes or until the pasta is nearly cooked (this will vary by pasta type).

4. Add the tomatoes, kidney beans, salt and honey and cook until everything is heated through.

5. Serve with a garnish of basil and some wholemeal bread.

The trick with this soup is to time the pasta so it does not overcook before the vegetables are cooked. If in doubt, wait until the vegetables are fully cooked. Undercook the pasta slightly as it will continue to cook after you remove the pot from the heat.

Wholemeal Shell Pasta

This pasta has a lovely mouth feel and the insides soak up liquid items which makes the dish interesting. Search out some good wholemeal pastas which have a lot more fibre and nutrients than white flour pasta.

SOUPS 111

Malaysian Laksa

MAKES 5 X 1 CUP SERVES

- 1 tablespoon oil
- 1 cup onion finely chopped (around 1 medium onion)
- 1 tablespoon ginger puree or finely chopped ginger
- 4 cloves garlic crushed or finely chopped
- 2 tablespoons lemongrass finely chopped (or frozen)
- 1 teaspoon sesame oil
- ½ cup red capsicum (bell pepper) very finely sliced (around ½ capsicum)
- ½ cup carrot very finely sliced (around ½ large carrot)
- 2 teaspoons coriander powder
- 1 teaspoon Thai red curry paste
- 3 tablespoons honey or date puree
- 400ml (12oz) tin coconut milk
- 1½ cups hot water
- 1 teaspoon salt
- 400g (12oz) block firm tofu diced
- 2 tablespoons lime juice (around 2 limes)
- ½ cup fresh mung bean sprouts
- garnish: ¼ cup fresh mint roughly chopped
- garnish: ½ cup fresh coriander (cilantro) roughly chopped
- garnish: lime wedges

One of my recipe testers Dawn (who has tasted many things in my books) commented that this was the best thing that I have ever made (and she is a foodie who gives me honest feedback)! It is the fragrant mixture of the mint, coriander and lime juice that takes this beautiful soup from excellent to awesome!!! So make sure you do not shortcut the garnishes on this one.

1. In a pan or pot, saute the oil, onion, ginger, garlic, lemongrass, sesame oil, capsicum and carrot for around 5 minutes or until the onion is soft.
2. Add the coriander and stir for around 30 seconds.
3. Mix the Thai red curry paste with a little water and add to the pot.
4. Add the honey, coconut milk, water and salt and heat until just about bubbling. Do not let the mixture boil or bubble.
5. Add the tofu and stir gently so as not to damage the tofu. It just needs to be gently heated and this will take around 2 minutes.
6. Add the lime juice.
7. Serve garnished with the limes, sprouts, mint, coriander and lime wedges.

This soup is also delicious served on rice noodles.

Citrus Squeezes

It is nice to give the person eating the food something to make their dish more flavoursome. It is part of the eating experience. So add some lime or lemon wedges to salads, hotpots or soups that would be nice with some extra zing.

SOUPS 113

Cauliflower makes a lovely smooth creamy soup. I have used nutritional yeast to give the flavour a bit of a kick. This soup tastes great but when I serve it at Revive it is polarising - with some people loving it, and some that dislike the taste of the nutritional flaked yeast - so you may want to go easy on this additive.

Curried Cauliflower Soup

MAKES 7 X 1 CUP SERVES

1½ cups onion diced (around 1 onion)

4 cloves garlic crushed or finely chopped

1 tablespoon oil

1 teaspoon mild curry powder

4 cups cauliflower roughly chopped

2 cups potato cubed (around 1 large)

4 cups boiling water

¾ cup cashew nuts raw

1¼ cups water

1 teaspoon salt

3 tablespoons nutritional flaked yeast

garnish: chopped chives

1. In a pot saute the onion, garlic and oil for around 5 minutes or until soft.
2. Add the curry powder and stir around for about 30 seconds.
3. Add the cauliflower, potato, water and salt and cook for around 20 minutes or until the potato is soft.
4. In a blender, blend the cashews and water until smooth. Add to the soup reserving a little for garnish.
5. Add the salt and flaked yeast.
6. Using a stick blender, blend the soup until creamy.
7. Serve with chives and reserved cashew cream on top.

I love the cheesy taste of the flaked nutritional yeast, however some people do not like the flavour so go cautiously if you are in doubt.

Fresh Chives

Another great herb to add a fresh flavour. Great with soups. They are so easy to grow in your garden too. You can have them thinly sliced, medium sliced, or they even work as long strips.

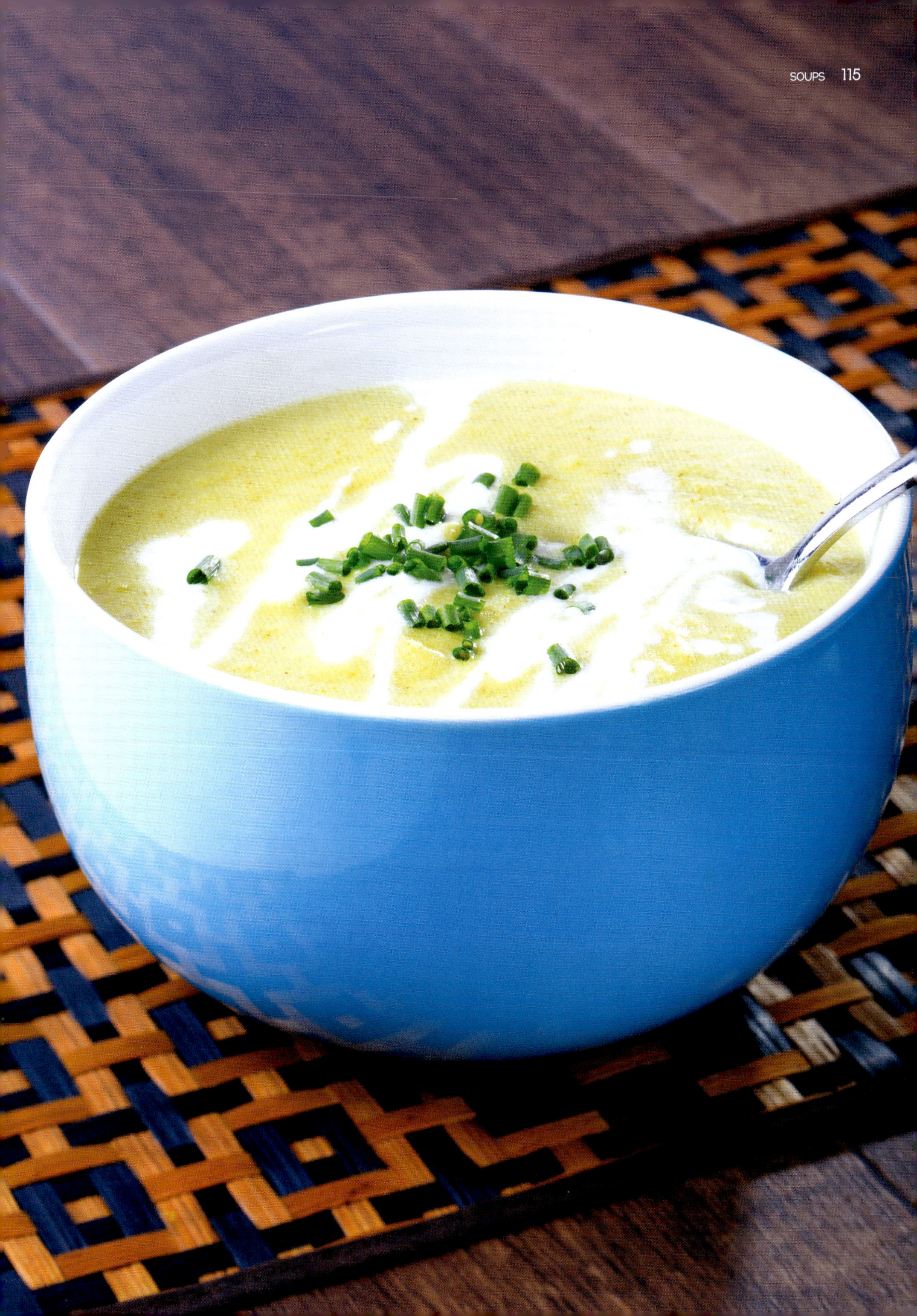

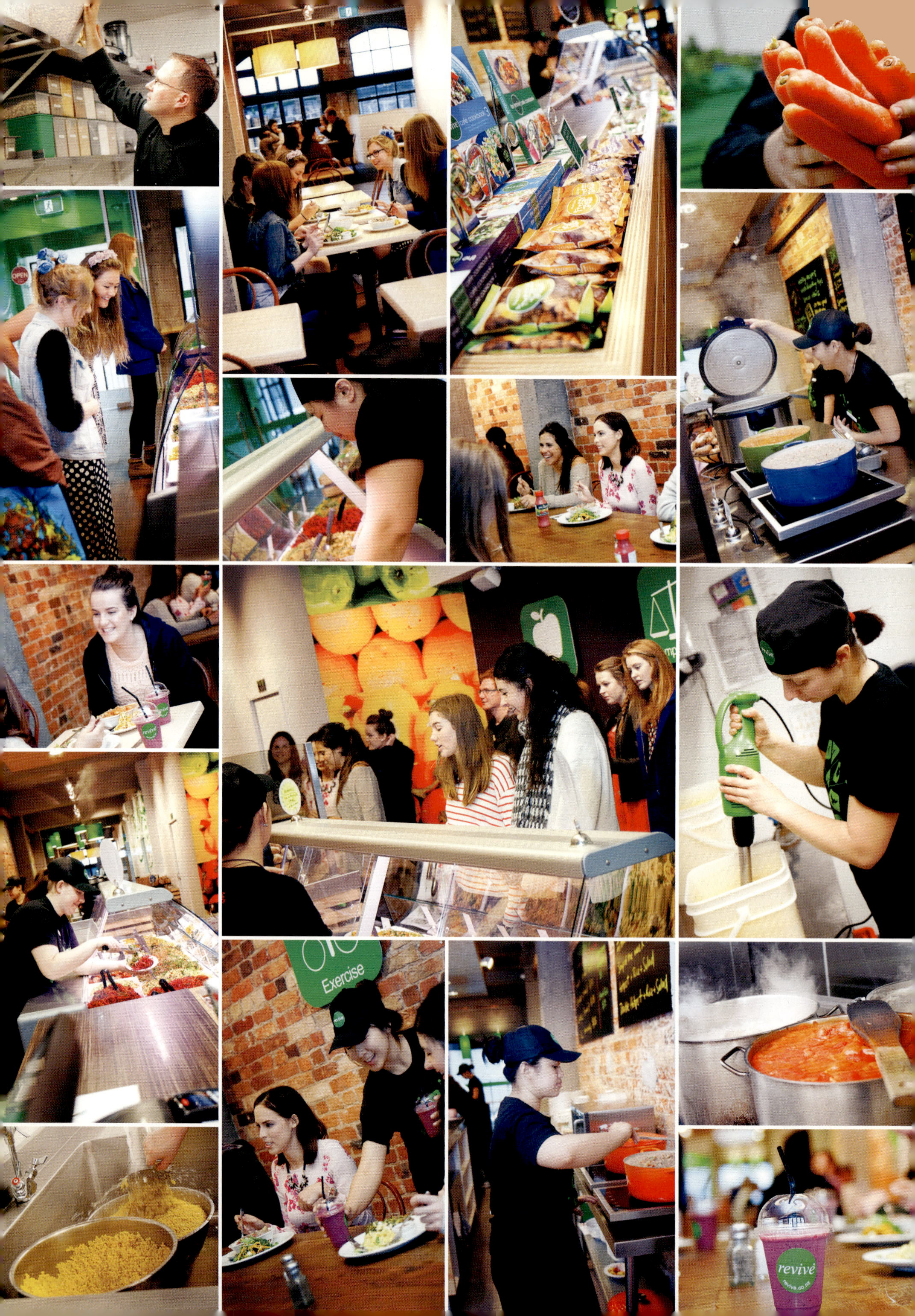
OPEN
Exercise
revivé

the ipad
ind you
or at
www.revive.co.nz
Sparkling Grape Juice or Apple $2.50
Organic Juices $4.20

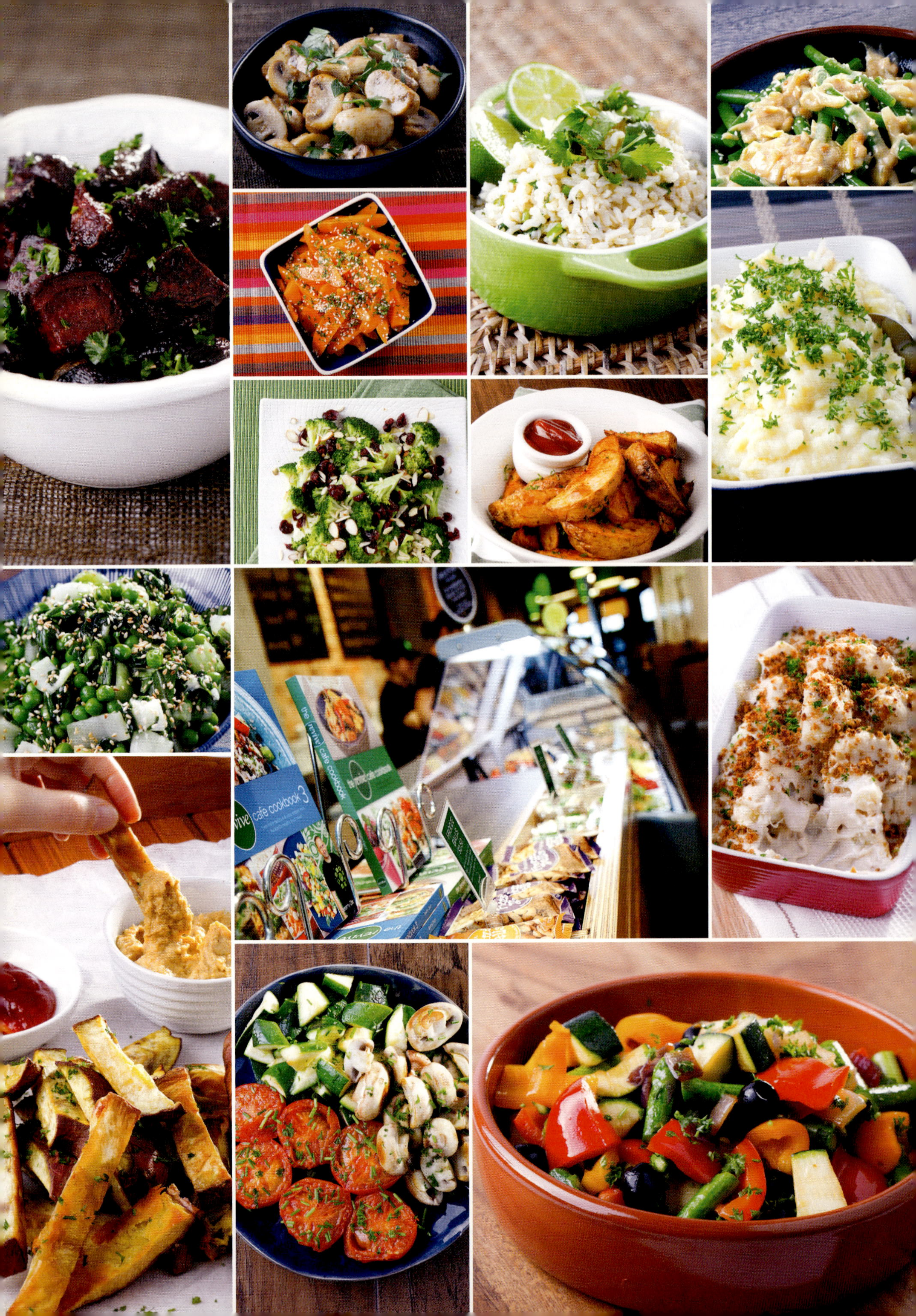
cafe cookbook 3
the revive cafe cookbook

Sides

Mediterranean Vegetables 120
Honey Glazed Carrots 122
Traditional Potato Mash 123
Sweet Potato Fries 124
Garlic Mushrooms 126
Broccoli & Cranberries 127
Satay Green Beans 128
Smoked Wedges 130
Green Pea Mingle 131
Cauliflower Cheese 132
Tangy Coriander Rice 134
Roasted Beetroot 135
Breakfast Vegetables 136

This is a great colourful dish that goes with any meal!

Mediterranean Vegetables

MAKES 4 X 1 CUP SERVES

1 tablespoon oil

4 cloves garlic finely chopped or crushed

1 cup red onion thickly diced (around 1 onion)

1 cup red capsicum (bell pepper) thickly diced (around 1 capsicum)

1 cup yellow capsicum (bell pepper) thickly diced (around 1 capsicum)

1 cup orange capsicum (bell pepper) thickly diced (around 1 capsicum)

1 cup courgette (zucchini) thickly diced (around 1 large courgette)

10 stalks asparagus cut into 2cm (1in) pieces

1 teaspoon salt

1 cup black olives

garnish: parsley

1. In a pan saute the oil, garlic and onion for around 3 minutes.

2. Add the other vegetables and saute for around 5 more minutes or until they are soft but still firm.

3. Sprinkle with salt and add the olives and stir.

This dish is best served straight after cooking. To save time, you can cut the vegetables in advance and cook just before serving.

SIDES 121

This is just cooked carrots with some easy additions. It can only takes a couple of ingredients to transform something from ordinary to awesome!

Honey Glazed Carrots

MAKES 4 X 1 CUP SERVES

4 cups carrots halved and diagonally sliced (approximately 3 large carrots)

1 tablespoon oil

1 tablespoons honey or date puree

¼ teaspoon salt

1 teaspoon sesame seeds

1 teaspoon parsley finely chopped

1. Put the sliced carrots in a pot with boiling water and cook for 5-7 minutes or until soft but still firm. Drain well.

2. Add oil, honey and salt and mix around.

3. Serve garnished with sesame seeds and chopped parsley.

A great winter side. Also great under many hotpot dishes.

Traditional Potato Mash

MAKES 4 X 1 CUP SERVES

4 cups potatoes skin on roughly chopped (around 2 large)

½ cup soy milk

½ teaspoon salt

1 tablespoon flaked nutritional yeast (optional)

garnish: parsley

1. Put the potatoes in a pot with boiling water and cook for around 15 minutes or until soft. Drain.

2. Mash with a potato masher. Leave some chunks of potato for interest rather than getting everything perfectly mashed.

3. Add remaining ingredients to the pot and stir well.

These are a great healthy winter dish. Sweet potato (kumara) has such a great flavour and needs very little oil (compared to potato chips) to make them taste amazing! Try these next time instead of normal fries. Thank you to my lovely wife Verity for being such a great hand model, although she somehow misunderstood my instructions and ended up eating all of the fries when I was not looking!

Sweet Potato Fries

MAKES 6 X 1 CUP SERVES

1½ kg (3lb) large red sweet potato (kumara) (around 3 large)

2 tablespoons oil

1 teaspoon salt

garnish: parsley

1. Slice the sweet potato into 1cm round discs. Then slice into chip shapes. There is no need to peel off the skin.

2. In a mixing bowl carefully mix the chips with the oil so they are evenly covered.

3. In an oven tray put some baking paper (for easy cleanup). Pour the chips on and arrange so they are evenly spaced.

4. Bake for 20-30 minutes at 180°C (350°F) or until just golden. Mix gently every 10 minutes to encourage even cooking.

5. Sprinkle the salt over the fries.

6. Serve with some hummus and tomato sauce (ketchup) and garnish with some finely chopped parsley.

You can use orange or gold sweet potato which are even sweeter however these fries will not hold together as well and you will have to be extra careful.

Many ovens are inaccurate with their temperatures. For a nice golden chip you need a high temperature and ideally on fan bake.

Cutting Fries

To make your own fries, cut your potato or kumara into large rounds. Then just slice into chip shapes. The same applies to potatoes.

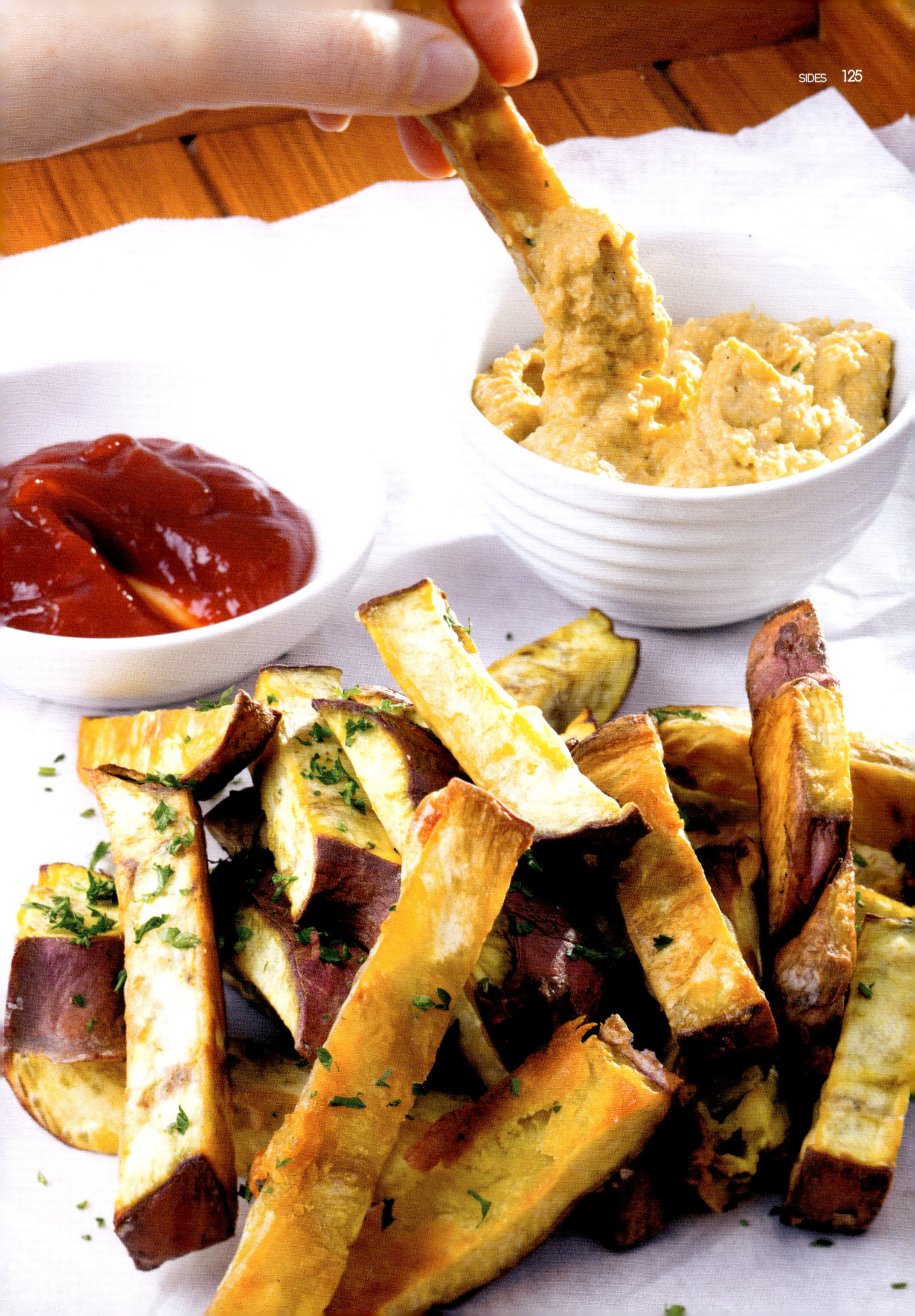

For a light dinner I will sometimes just have mushrooms on toast.

Garlic Mushrooms

MAKES 2 X 1 CUP SERVES

200g (6oz) button mushrooms halved (around 3 cups)

6 cloves garlic finely chopped or crushed

2 tablespoons oil

½ teaspoon salt

garnish: Italian parsley

1. In a pan saute the mushrooms, garlic and oil for around 5 minutes or until they are starting to shrink. You want the mushrooms cooked through but not shrivelled up.

2. Add the salt.

3. Serve with a garnish of Italian parsley.

A lovely side dish to make broccoli more exciting.

Broccoli & Cranberries

MAKES 4 X 1 CUP SERVES

4 cups broccoli florets
(around 1 medium broccoli)

¼ cup dried cranberries

¼ cup almonds sliced

1 teaspoon olive oil

¼ teaspoon salt

1. Put the broccoli in a pot with boiling water and cook for 3 minutes. The broccoli should still be firm but lose its raw taste.

2. Drain well.

3. Add the remaining ingredients to the pot and mix around.

If you want to serve this cold, make sure you rinse the broccoli in cold water straight away to stop it cooking and retain the dark green colour.

If you want to serve this dish warm, have everything chopped, measured and ready to go and put in the pot to cook just before serving.

Satay Green Beans

MAKES 4 X 1 CUP SERVES

SATAY SAUCE:

MAKES 2 CUPS

1½ cups onion finely diced (around 1 onion)

2 cloves garlic finely chopped or crushed

1 tablespoon ginger finely chopped or ginger puree

1 teaspoon oil

1 teaspoon turmeric powder

1 teaspoon cumin powder

½ cup peanut butter

1½ tablespoons honey or date puree

1 cup hot water

½ teaspoon salt

BEANS:

4 cups green beans

8 cups boiling water

garnish: white sesame seeds

1. In a pot or pan saute the onion, garlic, ginger and oil for around 5 minutes or until the onions are soft.
2. Add the spices to the pot and cook for around 30 seconds to activate the flavours.
3. Mix the peanut butter, honey and hot water in a cup. Add to the onion mix and add the salt.
4. Cook for around 5 minutes while stirring until it turns into a thick sauce.
5. Put the boiling water in another pot and boil rapidly.
6. Cut the ends off the beans and put in the water.
7. Cook for exactly 2 minutes. Drain immediately.
8. Serve the satay sauce on the beans with a garnish of sesame seeds.

Serve this dish hot straight away.

If serving this dish cold, cook the beans for 3 minutes and then put in very cold or iced water to stop the cooking process and retain the lovely green colour.

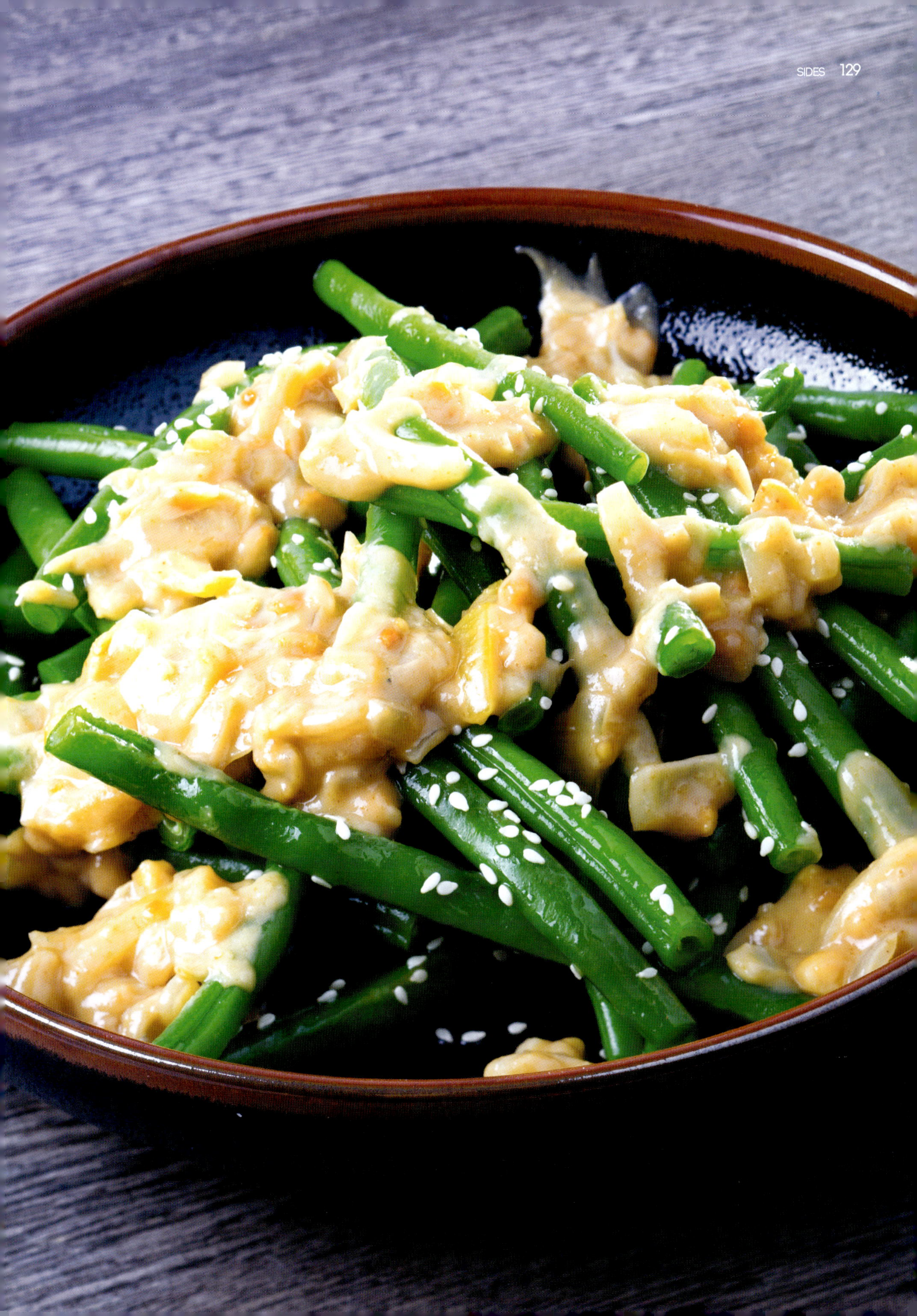

The wedges you buy in the supermarket are often coated in animal fats and artificial flavourings! Why do this when it is so easy to make healthy ones yourself?

Smoked Wedges

MAKES 4 X 1 CUP SERVES

4 small potatoes (around 4 cups) sliced into wedges

1 tablespoon oil

¾ teaspoon salt

2 teaspoons smoked paprika

garnish: parsley

1. In a bowl mix the potatoes with the oil, salt and smoked paprika.

2. Put on an oven tray and bake at 200°C (400°F) for around 30 minutes or until golden brown.

3. Serve with tomato sauce.

Just a few additions to frozen peas and you have an impressive side dish! Annelise my recipe tester for this dish said it was the first time her 3 children had ever eaten peas without coercion.

Green Pea Mingle

MAKES 4 X 1 CUP SERVES

2 teaspoons oil

2 cloves garlic finely chopped or crushed

3 cups frozen peas

3 cups silver beet (swiss chard) or spinach

¾ teaspoon salt

1 tablespoon honey or date puree

2 tablespoons toasted sesame seeds

1. In a pan or pot, saute the garlic, peas and silver beet for around 5 minutes or until the ingredients are heated.

2. Stir in the salt and honey.

3. Serve garnished with toasted sesame seeds.

Normally loaded with cheese, this healthy version tastes great and is so easy to make! You can use gluten free bread if you want this dish gluten free!

Cauliflower Cheese

MAKES 4 X 1 CUP SERVES

4 cups cauliflower cut into florets (around ½ head)

¼ cup wholemeal bread crumbs

garnish: parsley finely chopped

CHEESE SAUCE

¼ teaspoon salt

1 tablespoon nutritional yeast flakes

1 cup cashew nuts raw

1½ cups water

½ teaspoon arrowroot

1. Put the cauliflower in a pot of boiling water and simmer for around 6 minutes or until just softening. Drain well.

2. Combine the cheese sauce ingredients into a blender and blend until smooth. Pour into a pan or pot and heat gently while stirring until it thickens.

3. Put the cauliflower in a small baking dish, and cover with the cheese sauce. Sprinkle the bread crumbs on top.

4. Put in the oven and grill (broil) for around 4 minutes or until the bread crumbs are starting to brown.

5. Garnish with parsley.

To help stop the bread crumbs from burning, you can lightly spray the dish with oil before you grill it.

To make your own bread crumbs, just put a slice of bread in your food processor and process until fine. Do not over process and create bread dust as this will not look as good.

SIDES 133

If you want to add some zing to your rice try this recipe. You will be surprised how yummy it is. Great with any Mexican dishes or Thai curries.

Tangy Coriander Rice

MAKES 4 X ½ CUP SERVES

1 cup long grain brown rice

2 cups boiling water

¾ teaspoon salt

2 teaspoons olive oil

½ cup fresh coriander (cilantro) finely sliced (include the stalks)

¼ cup lime juice (around 2 limes)

1. In a pot combine the rice and boiling water and bring back to the boil.

2. Put the lid on and turn down the heat and simmer for around 25 minutes or until rice is soft and the water has disappeared. Do not stir.

3. Combine the remaining ingredients.

If you want the true flavour of beetroot you need to eat it raw or roasted rather than from a tin. Great as an ingredient for another dish or amazing eaten on its own.

Roasted Beetroot

MAKES 3 X 1 CUP SERVES

4 cups beetroot diced into 1 cm (½ in) cubes (around 2 large)

2 tablespoons oil

1 teaspoon salt

parsley for garnish

1. In a bowl mix the beetroot, oil and salt.

2. Tip onto a roasting tray and bake for 1 hour at 180°C (250°F) or until soft.

3. Serve with a garnish of parsley.

Put a layer of baking paper on the roasting tray to help with cleanup.

I love cooked breakfasts. And I do not mean hash browns and pancakes, but ones that have healthy vegetables. You can transform your cooked breakfasts with some simple freshly cooked vegetables. These go well with an omelette or scrambled tofu!

Breakfast Vegetables

MAKES 4 SERVES

10 medium button mushrooms

2 courgette (zucchini)

½ teaspoon salt

1 tablespoon oil

3 large tomatoes

garnish: chives

garnish: parsley

1. Cut the mushrooms in half. Make random cuts in the courgettes so they are all similar sizes. Cut the tomatoes in half.

2. In a pan saute the mushrooms and courgettes and 2 teaspoons of oil for around 5 minutes or until getting soft. Use half the pan for each vegetable. Add ¼ teaspoon salt.

3. In another pan saute the tomatoes with 1 teaspoon of oil for around 5 minutes (turning half way). Add ¼ teaspoon salt.

4. Garnish with chives and parsley.

Make sure you cook just before serving. If not, just undercook them and reheat them in a hot pan for a minute before serving.

Random Cut

My favourite cut. It looks random but it actually has some methodology to it. Cut the vegetable in to large strips (in the case of a courgette in half). Then make diagonal cuts, each time cutting into the last cut. The trick is to keep all the pieces approximately the same size.

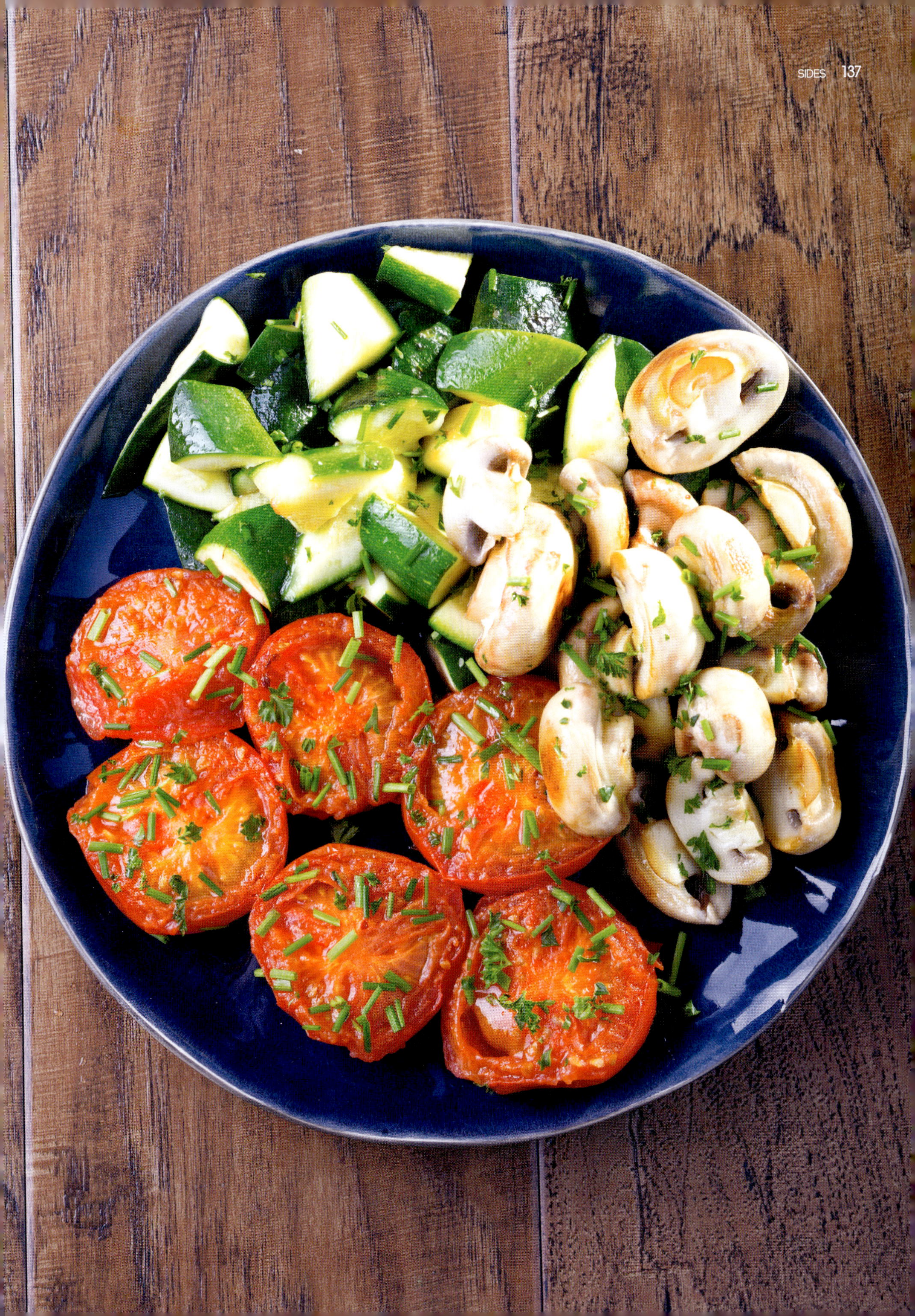

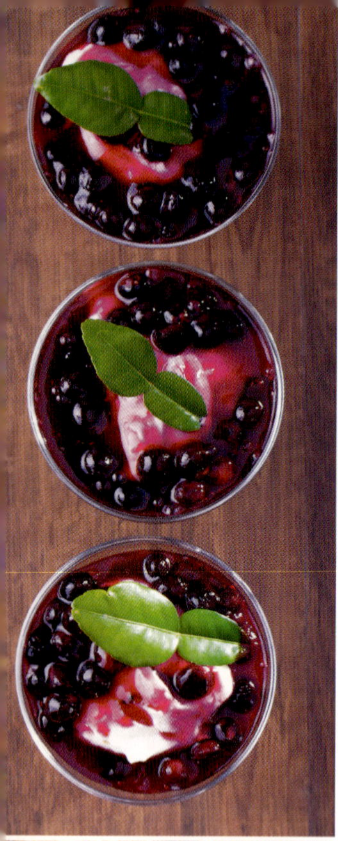
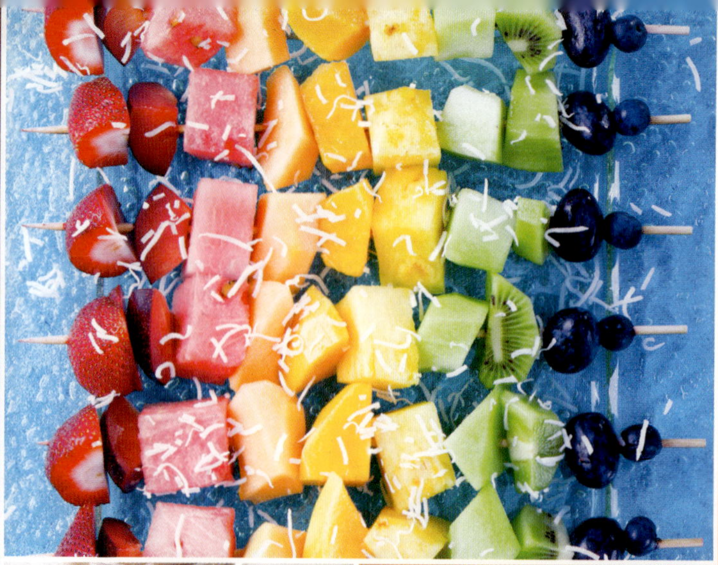
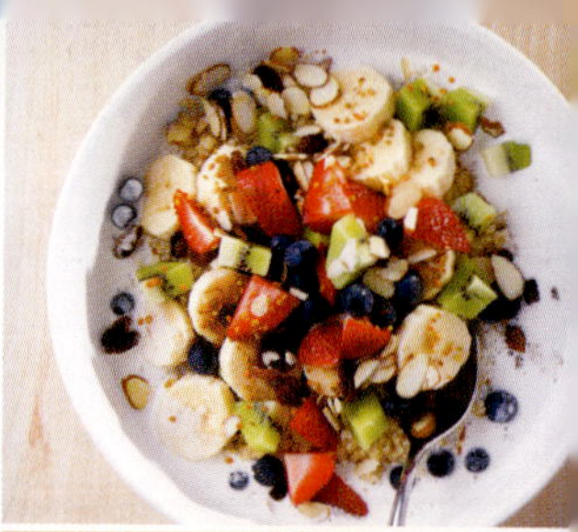
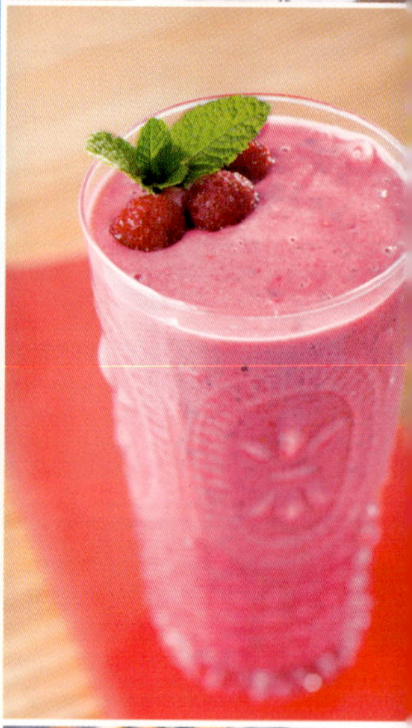
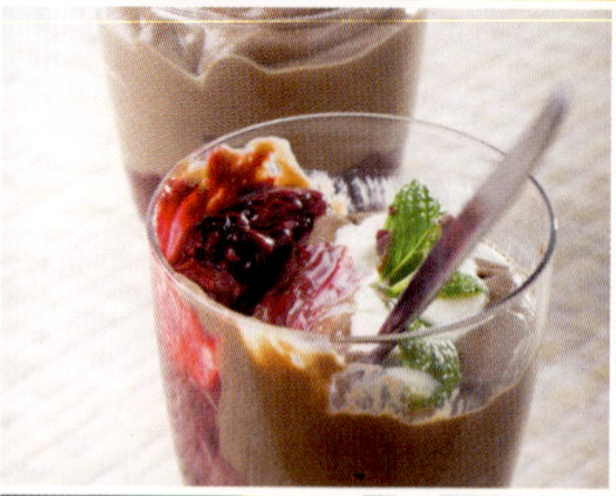
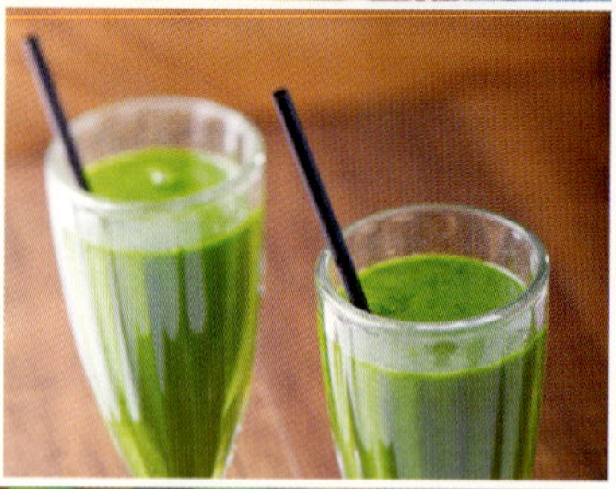
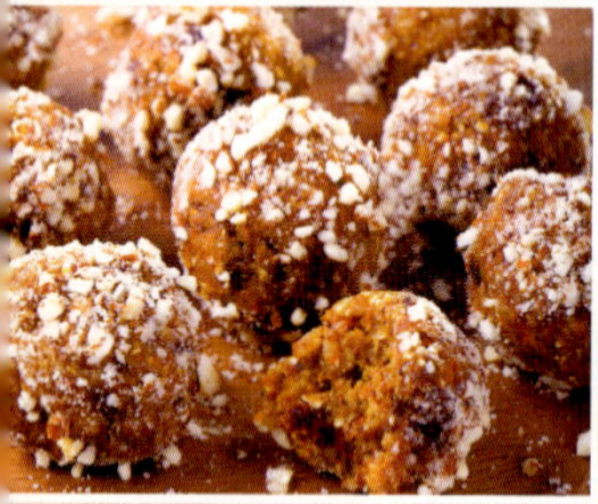
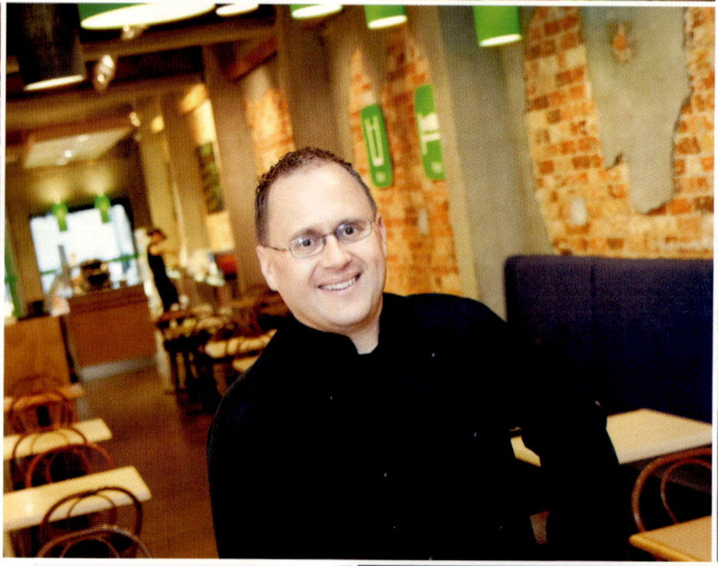
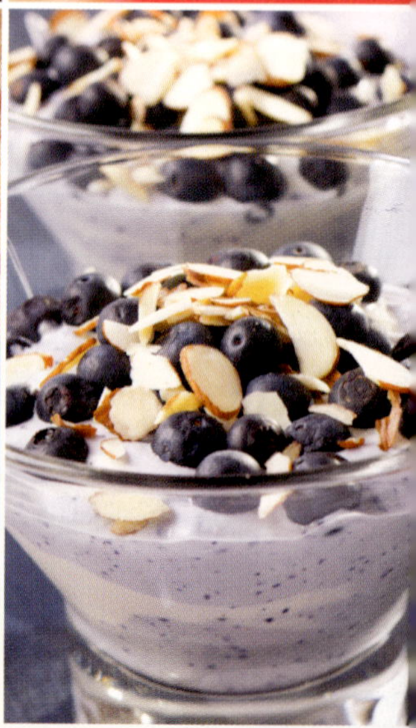
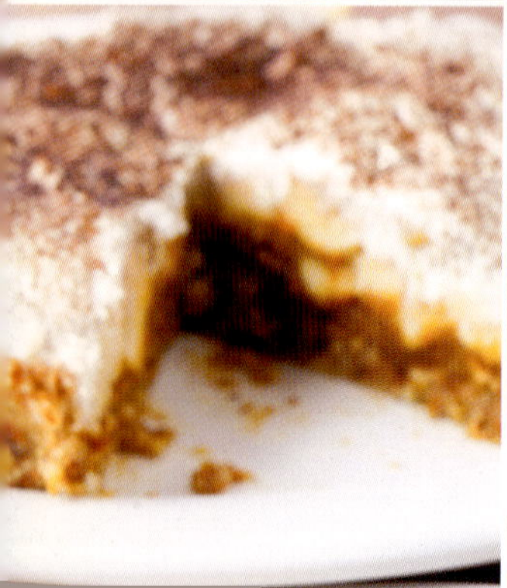
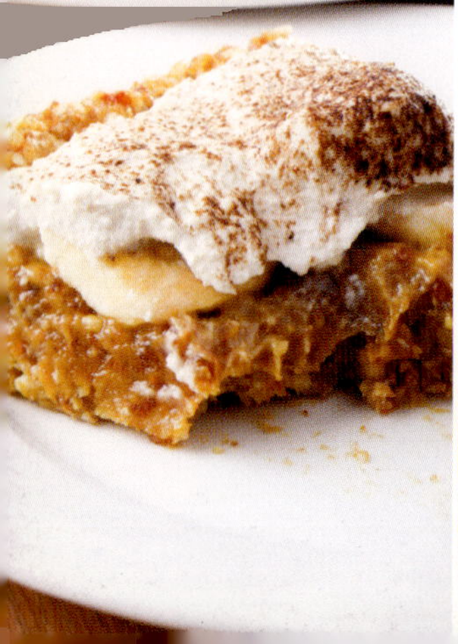
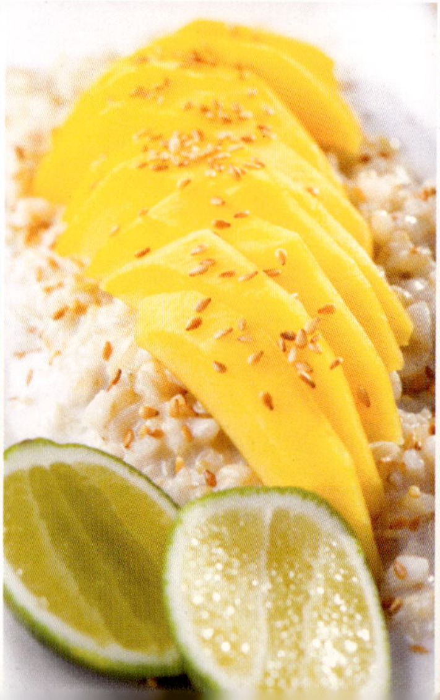
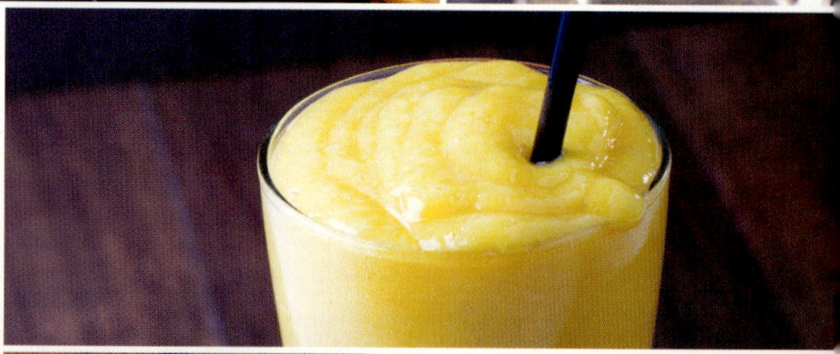
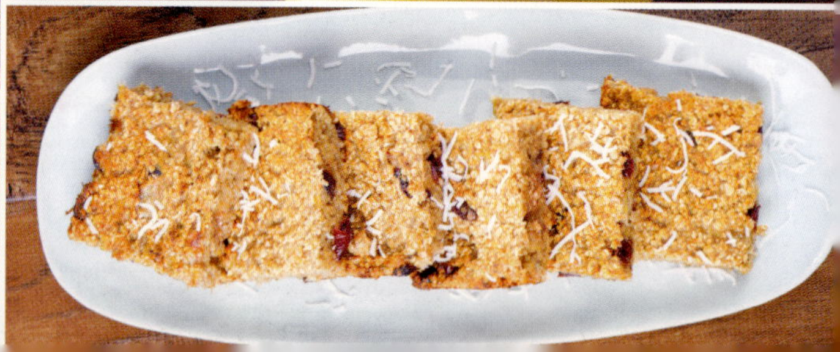

Sweet Things

Blueberry Parfait 140

Rainbow Fruit Kebabs 142

Healthy Banoffee Pie 144

Sticky Rice Mango 146

Chewy Cranberry Oat Slice 148

Blueberries & Cashew Cream 150

Jeremy's Fast Quinoa Breakfast 152

Moorish Carrot Cake Balls 154

Not Chocolate Mousse 156

Raspberry & Mint Smoothie 158

Sublime Green Smoothie 160

Mango & Lime Shake 161

This recipe has a lovely cheesecake-like texture and is an impressive dessert to serve up to people. You can use your favourite berries. I love frozen berries as you can enjoy them out of season.

Blueberry Parfait

MAKES 4 X 1 CUP SERVES

BASE:

2 cups cashew nuts raw

2 cups water

1 tablespoon honey or date puree

1 teaspoon agar agar

FRUIT TOPPING:

1 cup frozen or fresh blueberries

1 tablespoon honey

1 teaspoon arrowroot

½ cup cold water

1. Combine all of the base ingredients into a blender. Blend until smooth.
2. Pour into a pot or small frying pan and heat. Stir regularly until it is thickened.
3. Pour into 4 nice serving glasses.
4. In another pot heat the berries until they are defrosted.
5. Mix the arrowroot, water and honey in a cup and pour over the berries. Keep stirring until you have a nice thick mixture.
6. Pour the berry mixture over the base ingredients in the glasses.
7. Refrigerate for at least half an hour for it to firm up and cool.

This recipe is best when it is really well blended to make it smooth. You may have to blend for several minutes. Some lower powered blenders may struggle. You can also soak the cashews in water overnight to soften them which may help.

Agar Agar

This is a great natural gelatin alternative that comes from seaweed. When heated it turns things jelly-like. It is available ground up in powder from most Asian supermarkets - usually in small packets. You can also get it in its seaweed form but this will require it to be soaked in boiling water first.

SWEET THINGS 141

This is an awesome healthy dessert that kids especially love! They are actually quite time consuming so make sure you allow some time to cut and skewer them all. It is a great task to keep your children occupied and learn some new skills.

Rainbow Fruit Kebabs

MAKES 12 KEBABS

1 punnet strawberries

3 red plums

¼ small watermelon (red)

¼ rock melon (cantaloupe) (orange)

1 large mango

½ pineapple

½ honeydew melon (green)

2 kiwifruit

12 purple grapes

1 punnet blueberries

2 tablespoons shredded coconut

1. Skin the fruit and chop into 2cm (1in) chunks.

2. Push the fruit on the skewers.

3. Sprinkle with coconut.

You will have some leftover fruit pieces that are smaller or out of shape. Just make a fruit salad or smoothie out of these!

Use a nice sharp knife and handle the fruit gently to preserve the sharp edges that make it look appealing.

If you are not serving straight away cover with cling wrap, refrigerate and do not add the coconut.

If you use fruit that has been refrigerated overnight the fruit will look fresher longer at room temperature.

If you order the fruit like a rainbow you will get the best looking result! Red, orange, yellow, green, blue, indigo, violet.

Melons

Amazing for colour and taste great. The best fruit salads and kebabs are made with many different melons. Watermelon (red), rock melon (orange) and honeydew (green) work well together.

SWEET THINGS 143

I tasted a "real" banoffee pie around 10 years ago and was very impressed. Here is a healthy natural fruit and nut version. It is still a very concentrated dessert so you do not need much. But I think this is a good healthy replication given there is no chocolate, toffee, processed sugar or cream in the recipe!

Healthy Banoffee Pie

MAKES 10 SERVES

BASE
1 cup almonds raw
1 cup dates dried
1 cup cashew nuts raw
½ cup boiling water

FILLING
2 cups dates dried
½ cup peanut butter
1½ cups hot water

TOPPING
3 bananas sliced
1 cup cashew nuts raw
½ cup water

garnish: 1 tablespoon carob powder

1. Put the base ingredients in a food processor and process until it is clumping.
2. Tip into a round 25cm (8in) pie dish and press down and around the sides.
3. Combine the filling ingredients into the food processor (no cleaning required) and process until smooth.
4. Carefully spoon into the pie.
5. Slice the bananas and layer on the filling.
6. Clean the food processor and put the cashews and water in and process until you have a fine cream. Spoon this on top.
7. Sprinkle some carob powder on top.
8. Freeze for 1 hour for everything to firm up.
9. Serve.

In the unlikely event you have left-overs, store in the fridge to keep everything firm as it will soften at room temperature.

Cashew Pieces

Cashew nuts are a great ingredient for healthier creamy dishes. You can generally buy cashew pieces which work well for most recipes and are often half the price.

SWEET THINGS 145

This is a very popular dessert in Thailand that is available everywhere. It is normally sold with white rice and a lot of sugar so here is a healthier version!

Sticky Rice Mango

MAKES 1½ CUP SERVES

½ cup brown rice medium grain

1½ cups coconut milk

2 teaspoons honey or date puree

2 tablespoons lime juice (around 1 lime)

1 tablespoon sesame seeds

1 mango

garnish: half a lime

1. Combine the rice and coconut milk in a pot. Bring to the boil and turn down to a low heat and simmer for around 30 minutes with the lid on or until the rice is soft and liquid has been absorbed.

2. Take the lid off and let it sit for up to 10 minutes to thicken up.

3. Stir in the honey and lime juice.

4. Depending on how the rice has cooked you may want to add some more coconut milk to make a nice creamy mixture.

5. Put the sesame seeds in a hot non-stick frying pan and heat for around 2 minutes or until they are brown. Shake or stir the pan so they cook evenly while cooking.

6. Cut off 2 large cheeks from the mango, cut off the skin and then cut into smaller slices.

7. Serve the rice with the mango on top and a sprinkle of the toasted sesame seeds. Add some lime slices.

Mango

A lovely flavoursome fruit. Great in desserts and smoothies. I cut 2 large slices/cheeks off the 2 sides, cutting as close to the stone as possible. And then slice off the skin with a sharp knife.

SWEET THINGS **147**

The simple ingredients in this slice make it not only healthy and quick, but surprisingly delicious. You do not have to have white flour and processed sugar to have a delicious sweet treat!

Chewy Cranberry Oat Slice

MAKES 18 SERVES

4 ripe bananas (around 2 cups) mashed

2 cups rolled oats (fine/quick oats)

4 tablespoons date puree or honey

½ cup cranberries

¼ cup rice, oat or soy milk

1 teaspoon vanilla essence

1. Combine all ingredients into a bowl.
2. Press into a baking tray lined with baking paper.
3. Bake for 30 minutes at 180°C (350°F) or until firm.
4. Cool and cut into squares.

These will come out of the oven seemingly still soft and uncooked. However they will firm up after sitting for a while.

If your slices do not brown, switch the oven to grill (broil) mode and let the top cook for a couple of minutes to brown up.

Date Puree

My favourite sweetener that we use extensively at Revive. It is more natural than processed sugars, and one of the most inexpensive healthy sweeteners around. Just soak your dates in water (just covering) and when soft blend into a smooth puree. It will last in the fridge around 3 weeks.

SWEET THINGS 149

My friend Cherie talked me into helping her do a cooking demonstration around 10 years ago and presenting one of her recipes. It was my first demonstration ever! She uses a similar recipe as her healthy kids dessert that can be made quickly and in bulk. Cashew cream with blueberries is a great alternative to yoghurt or ice cream. Or you can present in glasses like the photo.

Blueberries & Cashew Cream

MAKES 4 X 1 CUP SERVES

2 cups cashew nuts raw

1½ cups water

1 tablespoon honey or date puree

⅛ teaspoon salt

½ teaspoon vanilla essence

2 cups blueberries

¼ cup sliced almonds

1. Put the cashews, water, honey, salt and vanilla essence in a food processor and process until smooth. Process longer than you think you need as you want cashew cream to form, rather than water and cashew pieces.

2. You may need to add a little more water so you have a consistency that is thick yet pourable.

3. Pour half the mixture into a bowl. Then put half of the blueberries in the food processor and process again.

4. You should now have half the cashew cream being white and half with a purple colour.

5. Layer the colours in serving glasses.

6. Sprinkle the remaining blueberries and sliced almonds on top.

This recipe works well with frozen berries and other berries like boysenberries and raspberries.

You can also go wild and have three different types of berry layers.

Dessert Glasses

Presentation is important for desserts. You possibly have some nice glasses like these buried in your cupboard not being used. Bring them out next time you have to make a dessert like this and wow your guests!

SWEET THINGS 151

Breakfast is my favourite meal of the day and I make sure it contains plenty of great food. I always have a lot of personal energy and this is due in part to a great breakfast and starting the day with a great attitude. This is a typical breakfast for me.

Jeremy's Fast Quinoa Breakfast

MAKES 2 SERVES

½ cup quinoa

1 cup boiling water

1 cup almond milk (or milk of your choice)

2 bananas chopped

1 cup blueberries (fresh or frozen)

2 kiwifruit chopped

½ cup chopped strawberries

½ teaspoon bee pollen

2 tablespoons raisins

2 tablespoons sliced almonds

1. In a pot combine the quinoa and boiling water and bring to the boil. Cover and simmer on low heat for around 12 minutes or until the water has disappeared and the quinoa is soft and fluffy. This should yield 1¼ cups of cooked quinoa.

2. Add milk and top with remaining ingredients.

Warning - you will have a lot of energy after this breakfast!

This recipe assumes you are cooking up the quinoa in the morning. In reality I will cook up a larger batch the night before that will last me several mornings of breakfasts. If I am doing this, in the winter I will quickly warm the cooked quinoa with the milk in a pot on the stove.

Bee Pollen

This is one of my favourite "superfoods". It is a great natural energy enhancer and I have it on my breakfast most mornings.

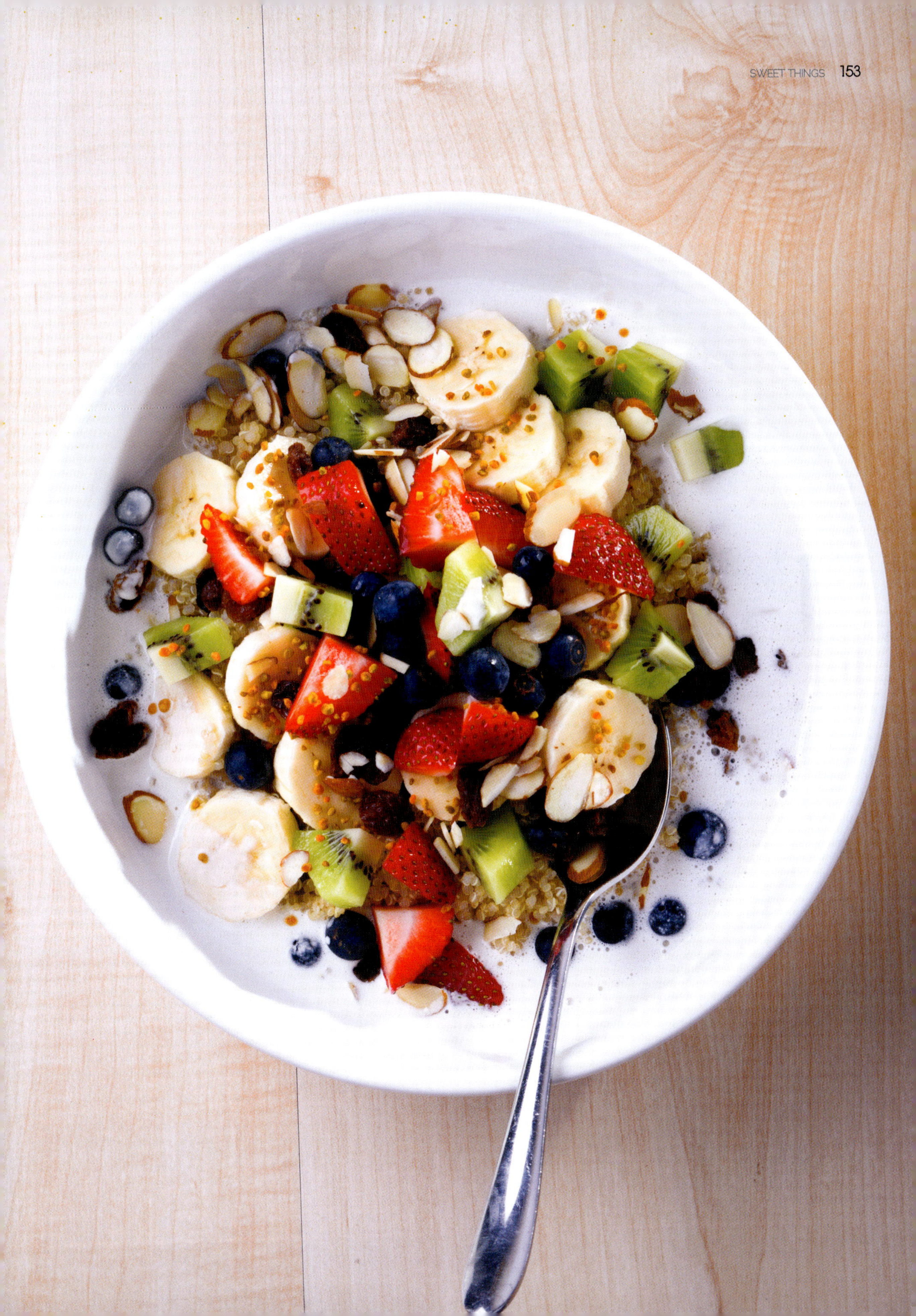

I was looking to add a carrot cake to this book and was struggling to get a healthy recipe to work so I decided to put the healthful ingredients into a ball and it worked! These are very yummy. They will theoretically keep in the refrigerator for around a week. Although the chance of this happening is quite small given how good they taste.

Moorish Carrot Cake Balls

MAKES 12 MEDIUM BALLS

½ cup dried dates

½ cup sultanas

¼ cup almonds

1 cup rolled oats (oatmeal) (fine or whole)

1 cup carrots (finely diced or grated) (around 1 carrot)

½ cup almonds

¼ teaspoon cinnamon

¼ teaspoon nutmeg

½ teaspoon clove powder

1. Soak the dates and sultanas in some boiling water for 5 minutes to soften them. Drain.

2. Put the almonds in a food processor and blend briefly so you have small pieces. You do not want to over blend and have almond dust. Pour into a bowl.

3. The almonds are done first so you can use the food processor for 2 jobs without cleaning inbetween.

4. Combine the dried fruit, oats, carrots, whole almonds, and spices in the food processor and process until it is a consistent mixture. You may have to scrape down the sides.

5. Scoop out the mixture and make balls to the size of your choosing (I like 1½ tablespoon sized balls.

6. Roll in the bowl with the almond pieces.

The balls will firm up in the refrigerator.

Cinnamon

A fragrant spice that is great for sweet things! It is quite overpowering so I generally err on adding less than more. It combines well with nutmeg and clove powder like in this recipe.

SWEET THINGS 155

There are many "healthy" chocolate mousse recipes around however most of them use large amounts of coconut oil or cream and taste very rich and are high in fat. When I tried tofu I thought it would not taste good at all, however the honey and carob overpowers this for a mousse that is delicious and not too rich. Also this mousse contrasts amazingly with the berry coulis mix on the bottom.

Not Chocolate Mousse

MAKES 4 X 1 CUP SERVES

MOUSSE

5 tablespoons carob powder

300g (10oz) firm tofu

4 tablespoons honey or date puree

½ avocado

¼ teaspoon salt

¾ cup water

BERRY COULIS

1½ cups frozen boysenberries (or berries of your choice)

¼ cup cold water

1 teaspoon arrowroot

CREAM

¼ cup cashew nuts raw

¼ cup water

garnish: mint leaves

1. Put all of the mousse ingredients into a blender and process until smooth and silky. You will need to add enough water to keep the mixture moving but not too much to make it too liquid. Make sure you have a smooth mixture - if you see flecks of tofu keep processing.

2. In a small pan heat the boysenberries until they are just thawed.

3. Mix together the water and arrowroot in a cup. Pour over the berries and continue to heat. Stir until it thickens up. Do not overstir and crush the berries as you still want to retain the shape of the whole berries.

4. In a 250ml (8oz) glass pour in layers of berry coulis and the mousse. Make sure you divide evenly into 4 so you have enough.

5. In a blender, blend the cashew nuts and water until smooth.

6. Garnish with the cashew cream and some mint.

If you add too much water and your mixture is too runny, you can add some more tofu to thicken it up.

Frozen berries are very convenient and inexpensive out of season. However if you have seasonal fresh berries just add these cold and do not make the coulis mix.

SWEET THINGS 157

The tartness of raspberries combined with the sweetness of the banana and date puree give an awesome smoothie. I prefer smoothies with one berry (rather than mixed berries) so you can enjoy a single unique flavour.

Raspberry & Mint Smoothie

MAKES 2 X 300ML (10OZ)
SERVES

1 cup milk of your choice (soy, almond, rice, oat)

2 cups frozen raspberries

½ cup fresh mint

2 tablespoons honey or date puree

1 large ripe banana

1. Put all ingredients into a blender and blend.

Frozen Raspberries

A lovely berry that is great to have in the freezer. It is one of the more tart berries so it works well with a lot of sweetness added. It is also good when crumbled and used as a sprinkle on healthy cheesecakes, fruit crumbles and other healthy sweets.

SWEET THINGS **159**

Green smoothies have a lot of vitamin C and other nutrients! I know many people who have overcome illness and increased their energy by having a green smoothie a day. You can add any fruits or leafy green vegetables that you like.

Sublime Green Smoothie

MAKES 3 X 1 CUP SERVES

2 kiwifruit

1 cup pineapple diced

1 banana

1 orange

optional: 1 cup ice

2 cups pressed down spinach

2 cups pressed down silverbeet

1. Put all ingredients into a blender and blend until smooth. You may have to add a little water to make it free flowing.

Put the leafy greens at the top of the blender to enable the fruit at the bottom to become liquid.

You can use any leafy greens you like for this smoothie.

While travelling in Asia I loved the "fruit shakes" that appear in many places. Here is a delicious mango based one. You can use fresh mango or some supermarkets stock frozen mango pieces which are excellent.

Mango & Lime Shake

MAKES 2 X 1 CUP SERVES

1 cup mango pieces (around 1 medium mango)

1 ripe banana

1 tablespoon lime juice

1 tablespoon honey or date puree

optional if using fresh mango:
1 cup ice

1. Put all ingredients into a blender and blend until smooth. You may have to add a little water to make it free flowing.

Depending on the sweetness of your mangos you can leave out or increase the honey or date puree.

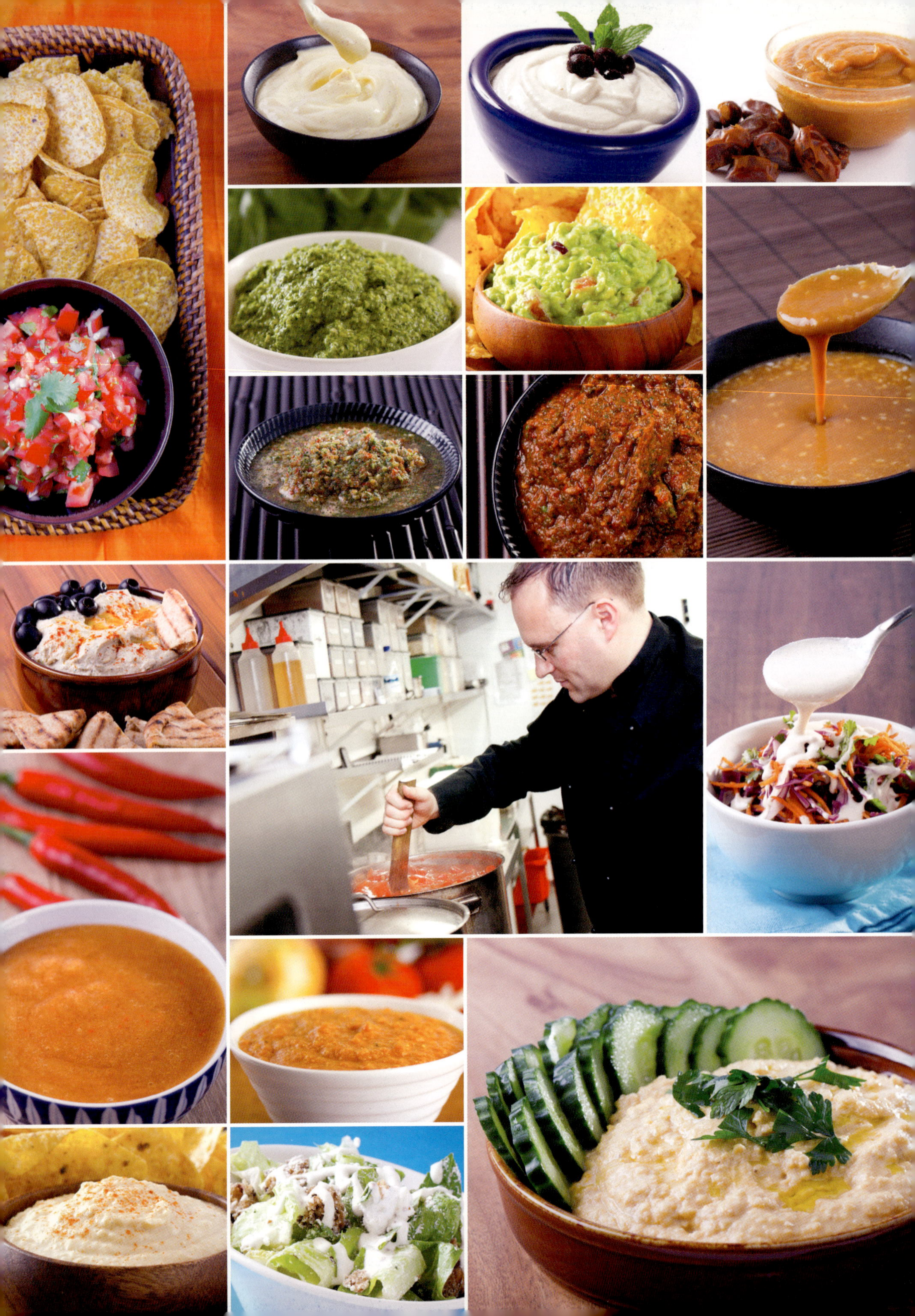

Flavour Boosters

Mexican Salsa 164

Asian Sesame Miso Dressing 165

Moroccan Butternut Hummus 166

Homemade Sweet Chilli Sauce 168

Baba Ganoush 170

Tahini Dressing 171

Homemade Thai Red Curry Paste 172

Homemade Thai Green Curry Paste 173

Revive Aioli 174

Italian Tomato Sauce 174

Basil Pesto 175

Date Puree 175

Tofu Mayo 176

Cashew Cream 176

Classic Hummus 177

Avocado Guacamole 177

This salsa is amazing. It is filled with so many flavoursome ingredients like garlic, fresh chilli and lime juice which combine well with the tomato. It is great with corn chips or works well with many meals.

Mexican Salsa

MAKES 2½ CUPS

2 cups finely chopped ripe tomatoes (around 4 tomatoes)

2 cloves garlic finely chopped or crushed

¼ cup lime juice (around 1 lime)

¼ cup red onion very finely chopped (around ¼ onion)

1 red chilli finely diced (optional)

½ cup finely chopped coriander (cilantro)

½ teaspoon salt

1. Combine all ingredients in a bowl and stir gently.
2. Serve straight away.

I check the potency of my chilli by cutting a small sliver and dabbing it on my tongue. It is hard to tell visually. Some will be as weak as a capsicum (bell pepper) and some will be very very hot. In general the smaller the chilli the hotter it will be.

To chop tomatoes finely you need a very sharp knife or use a serrated knife.

This quick dressing adds a nice Asian flavour to anything it touches.

Asian Sesame Miso Dressing

MAKES ½ CUP

2 tablespoons miso paste

2 tablespoons honey or date puree

1 tablespoon sesame oil

1 tablespoon ginger puree or finely chopped

4 tablespoons lemon juice

1 teaspoon white sesame seeds

1. Mix all ingredients in a cup.

Miso paste is fermented soy bean paste. You can find it in Asian and whole food stores.

This takes my basic hummus recipe and supercharges it with some extra ingredients. The caramalised onion and butternut makes this dip very sweet and flavoursome.

Moroccan Butternut Hummus

MAKES 4 CUPS

3 cups cubed butternut squash or pumpkin

1 tablespoon oil

1½ cups finely diced onion (around 1 large onion)

1 teaspoon oil

2 cloves garlic finely chopped or crushed

1 teaspoon cumin

1 teaspoon coriander

1 teaspoon salt

400g (12oz) tin chickpeas (garbanzo beans)

2 tablespoons lemon juice

2 tablespoons tahini

½ cup water (possibly more)

1. Combine the butternut and 1 tablespoon of oil on an oven tray and bake at 180°C (350°F) for around 15 minutes or until soft.

2. In a pan saute the onion, 1 teaspoon of oil and garlic for around 5 minutes or until onion is clear.

3. Stir in the cumin and coriander and heat for around 1 minute to activate the spices.

4. Put all ingredients into a food processor and process until creamy. You may need to add more water.

5. Add a drizzle of olive oil and some coriander to garnish. Serve with some fresh raw vegetables or crackers.

Hummus will keep in the refrigerator for around 3-4 days.

For a different texture add the onion to the food processor after blending.

You can also use a blender (liquidiser) or stick blender - however you will most likely need to add more water to keep the blades blending and will result in a runnier hummus.

FLAVOUR BOOSTERS | 167

Sweet chilli sauce is a chef's secret ingredient. When a recipe need a little lift, this will add sweetness, saltiness and hotness instantly. It rounds out all the flavours. There are a handful of brands that are not full of preservatives and flavour enhancers. But these are still quite high in sugar - which is not too bad if you are using small amounts. However the best solution is to make your own with this healthy recipe!!!

Homemade Sweet Chilli Sauce

MAKES 1½ CUPS

- ½ cup dates
- ¾ cup hot water
- 4 cloves garlic
- 2 red chilli (with seeds)
- 4 tablespoons lemon juice
- 1 teaspoon salt
- 1 tablespoon arrowroot
- ¼ cup cold water

1. Put the dates and hot water into the blender jug and let sit for around 5 minutes or until they have softened.

2. Add the garlic, chilli, lemon juice and salt and blend until smooth.

3. Pour the sauce into a pot and cook until bubbling. Simmer for another 5 minutes.

4. In a cup mix the arrowroot and ¼ cup of cold water and stir into the sauce. It should thicken quickly.

To make things like this last well in the refrigerator it is important to have exceptionally clean pots, blenders, hands and knives to minimise any bacteria. Also cool down for 30 minutes and then refrigerate.

The most difficult thing about making this sauce is the hotness of the chilli. All are different. I usually cut off a tiny piece and put on my tongue to determine how hot it is and how many I will use.

FLAVOUR BOOSTERS 169

I love this traditional Turkish dip made with eggplant!

Baba Ganoush

MAKES 1½ CUP SERVES

2 eggplants (aubergines) large
4 tablespoons tahini
4 tablespoons lemon juice
2 cloves garlic
½ teaspoon cumin
¾ teaspoon salt
¼ cup parsley
½ teaspoon smoked paprika
garnish: olives
garnish: smoked paprika
garnish: oilive oil

1. Put the whole eggplant into the oven and bake at 180°C (350°F) for 15-20 minutes or until they are soft and starting to sag in the middle. Cool and scoop out the flesh (do not use the skins).

2. Put all ingredients into a blender and blend until smooth.

3. Serve with wholemeal pita bread and a garnish of olives, oil and smoked paprika.

This is a great lower fat alternative to aioli as it has no oil added.

Tahini Dressing

MAKES 1 CUP

4 tablespoons tahini

4 tablespoons lemon juice

½ teaspoon salt

1 large clove garlic

1 tablespoon honey or 4 dates (soaked)

4 tablespoons water

1. Put all ingredients into a blender and blend until smooth.

If using dates, soak them in boiling water for 5 minutes and drain before blending. This will soften them up.

Using honey will give a white dressing, while date puree will make this dressing a light brown colour.

I often use the store-made curry pastes. These give a good result and are quick. However if you want that extra authentic Thai taste in your dishes and have a little more time, a couple of minutes spent making your own curry paste is worth it.

Homemade Thai Red Curry Paste

MAKES 1½ CUPS

2 cloves garlic

2 tablespoons ginger

1 teaspoon chilli paste or 2 whole chillie

1 cup fresh coriander (cilantro) (pressed down)

6 kaffir lime leaves (optional)

2 stalks lemongrass roughly chopped or 2 tablespoons frozen pieces

2 tablespoons honey or date puree

½ teaspoon salt

¼ cup lemon juice

½ cup tomato puree

1 teaspoon cumin powder

1 teaspoon coriander powder

1. Put all of the curry paste ingredients into a food processor and blend well.

2. Add to any curry or salad.

Use all of the coriander stalks (excluding the roots) as these provide awesome flavour.

Every homemade curry paste will be different so make sure you test the flavour in your dish before you serve.

FLAVOUR BOOSTERS

This is similar to the red curry paste except leaving out some ingredients. Generally green pastes are hotter.

Homemade Thai Green Curry Paste

MAKES 1 CUP

2 cloves garlic

2 tablespoons ginger

1 tablespoon chilli paste or 2 whole chilli

1 cup fresh coriander (cilantro) (pressed down)

6 kaffir lime leaves (optional)

2 stalks lemongrass roughly chopped or 2 tablespoons frozen pieces

2 tablespoons honey or date puree

½ teaspoon salt

¼ cup lemon juice

2 tablespoons sesame oil

1. Put all of the curry paste ingredients into a food processor and blend well.

2. Add to any curry or salad.

You can increase or decrease the chilli content for your taste buds!

These curry pastes will keep in the refrigerator for around 2 weeks if sealed.

Revive Aioli

MAKES 3 CUPS

½ cup soy milk

1 tablespoon cider vinegar or lemon juice

3 cloves garlic

1 tablespoon whole grain mustard

½ teaspoon salt

2 cups oil

½ to 1 cup room temperature water

1. Select a blender, food processor or stick blender.
2. Blend all ingredients (except oil and water).
3. While blending, slowly add oil and then add water at end until desired consistency is reached.

When making dressings you need to ensure that all items are at room temperature, and that you add the oil slowly.

Aioli will last 2-3 weeks in your refrigerator.

Italian Tomato Sauce

MAKES 6 CUPS

1½ cups onion chopped (around 1 onion)

4 cloves garlic crushed

2 tablespoons oil

3 x 400g (12oz) tins tomatoes

¾ teaspoon salt

1 teaspoon mixed dried herbs

3 tablespoons honey or date puree

1. In a pot saute onion, garlic and oil until clear.
2. Add remaining ingredients and cook until bubbling.
3. Blend all the sauce with a stick blender.

If you really like garlic add twice as much for a great garlic taste.

FLAVOUR BOOSTERS

Basil Pesto

MAKES 2 CUPS

1 large bunch fresh basil (around 125g/4oz)

½ cup oil

1 cup cashew nuts raw

½ teaspoon salt

¼ cup lemon juice (around 2 lemons)

2 cloves garlic

1. Put all ingredients into a food processor and blend until it is well mixed, but there are still some nut pieces showing.

2. You can use a blender or stick blender but you will have to add a little more oil or water to make the mixture turn.

For a different flavour you can use almonds or walnuts instead of cashew nuts.

Traditionally pesto uses pine nuts - however these are around 4 times the price of almonds and cashews.

Use coriander (cilantro) instead of basil for a different pesto.

Date Puree

MAKES 2 CUPS

2 cups pitted dried dates

2 cups boiling water

1. Put dates in boiling water for 5 minutes to soften.

2. Put the water and dates in blender and blend well until you have a smooth paste.

3. If you hear date stones (as they occasionally come through), sieve the puree.

4. Put into an air-tight container and store in the refrigerator.

You can use cold water to soak the dates - however it will take several hours for them to soften.

Date puree will last 2-3 weeks in your refrigerator.

THE RECIPES ON THESE PAGES HAVE BEEN REPEATED FROM "THE REVIVE CAFE COOKBOOK 1 & 2"

Tofu Mayo

MAKES 2 CUPS

2 cups (350g/10oz) firm tofu

5 tablespoons lemon juice

1 tablespoon whole grain mustard

1 clove garlic

1 tablespoon honey or date puree

1 teaspoon salt

1. Put all ingredients into a blender, food processor or use a stick blender and blend until smooth.

2. If it is too thick and stalls the blender you can add a little more water.

You can also add a little turmeric if you want a more yellow colour.

As this contains fresh tofu, this will keep in the refrigerator for only a couple of days so use up quickly.

Cashew Cream

MAKES 1½ CUPS

1 cup cashew nuts raw

½ cup water

optional: 2 tablespoons honey or date puree

optional: 1 drop of vanilla essence

1. Put all ingredients into a blender or use a stick blender.

2. Blend well until smooth.

3. You may need to add more water to achieve the consistency you are after.

The cream is very nice with just water and cashew nuts, however add the vanilla and honey if you want a sweet version.

To make this amazing add a tin of pears (with juice) instead of the water and you have cashew and pear cream.

Classic Hummus

MAKES 3 CUPS

2 x 400g (12oz) cans of chickpeas (garbanzo beans)

½ teaspoon of salt

2 cloves of garlic chopped or crushed

2 tablespoons tahini (ground hulled sesame seed paste)

½ cup water

4 tablespoons lemon juice

1. Put all ingredients in food processor and blend until smooth. You can also use a stick blender or a regular blender however you may have to add more water to keep it flowing.

2. Taste. Note that all batches vary in flavour as salt, chickpeas and lemon juice always have different flavours and consistency.

3. Add water/oil/salt as needed. You should be able to taste every ingredient slightly, with not too much of any ingredient coming through.

My previous recipes have had oil in hummus - however I now just replace with water.

Avocado Guacamole

MAKES 1-2 CUPS

1 large or 2 medium avocados (ripe)

1 small tomato finely diced

¼ red onion finely diced

1 clove garlic chopped or crushed

2 tablespoons freshly squeezed lemon juice

¼ teaspoon salt

optional: 2 tablespoons sweet chilli sauce

1. Halve, carefully remove the stones and skin of the avocado and put in a mixing bowl. Mash with a fork.

2. Add all other ingredients and mix together.

I prefer not too much onion and tomato in my guacamole, however if you want more texture put in more onion and tomato.

THE RECIPES ON THESE PAGES HAVE BEEN REPEATED FROM "THE REVIVE CAFE COOKBOOK 1, 2 & 3"

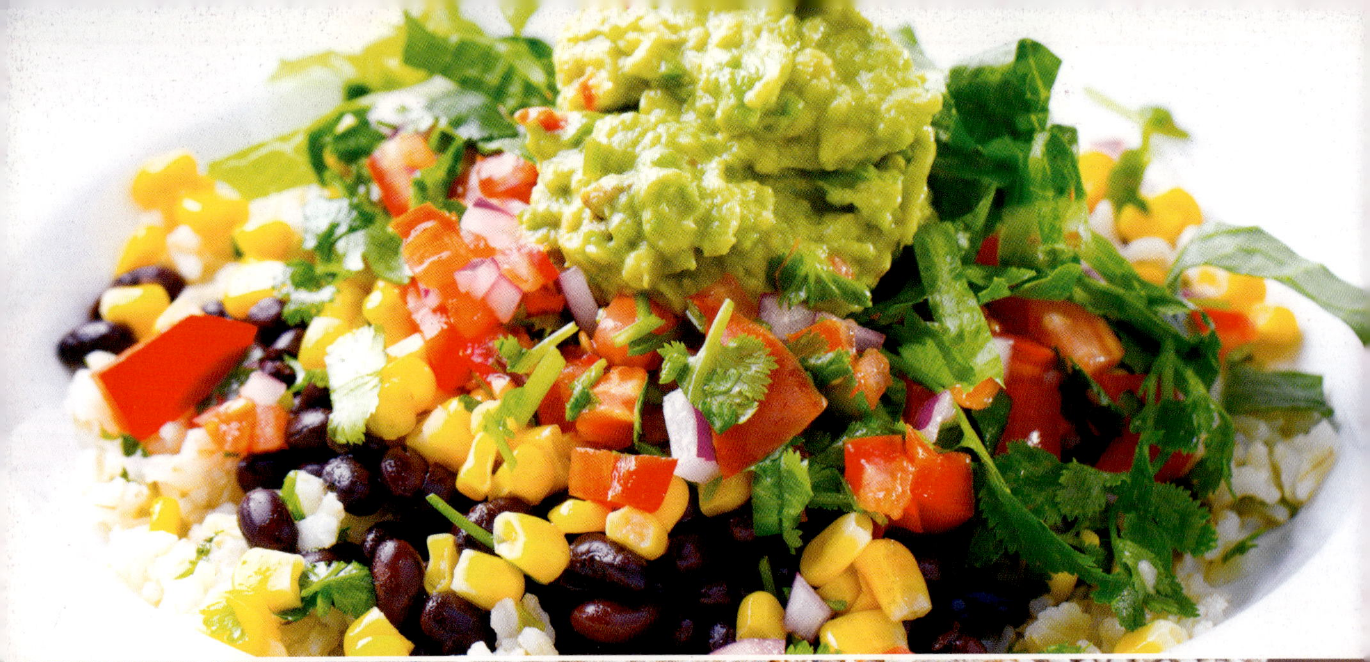
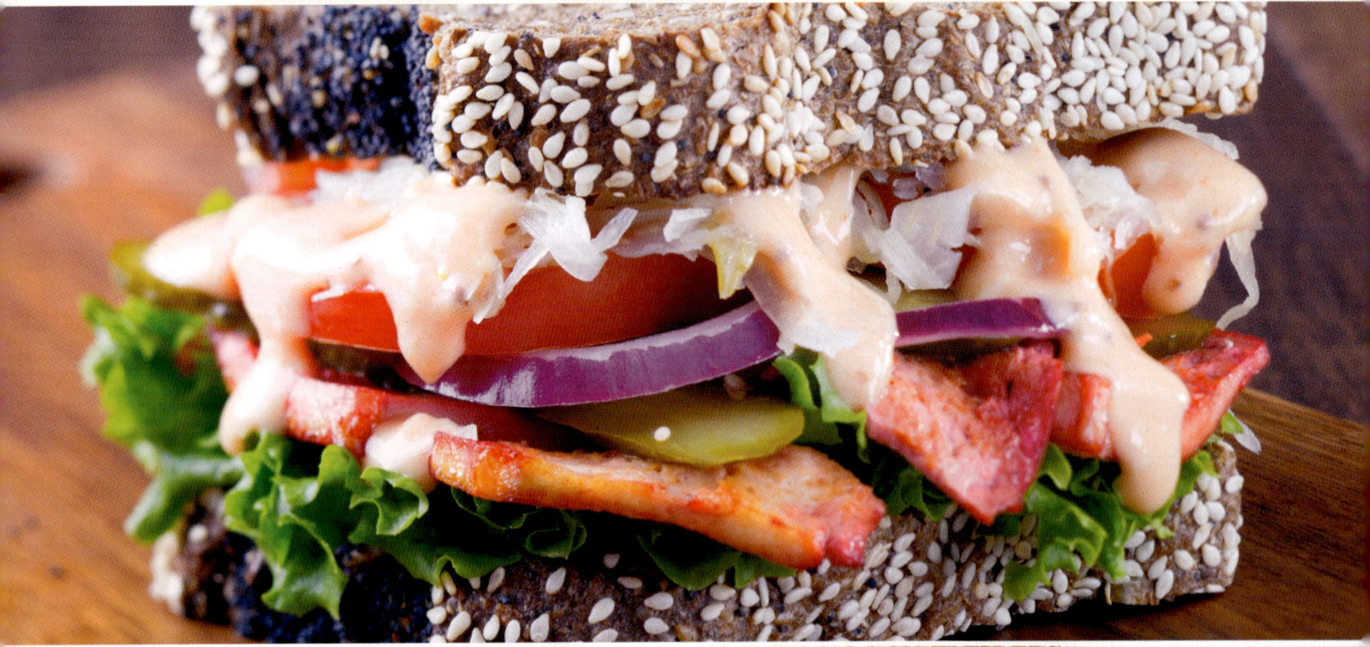
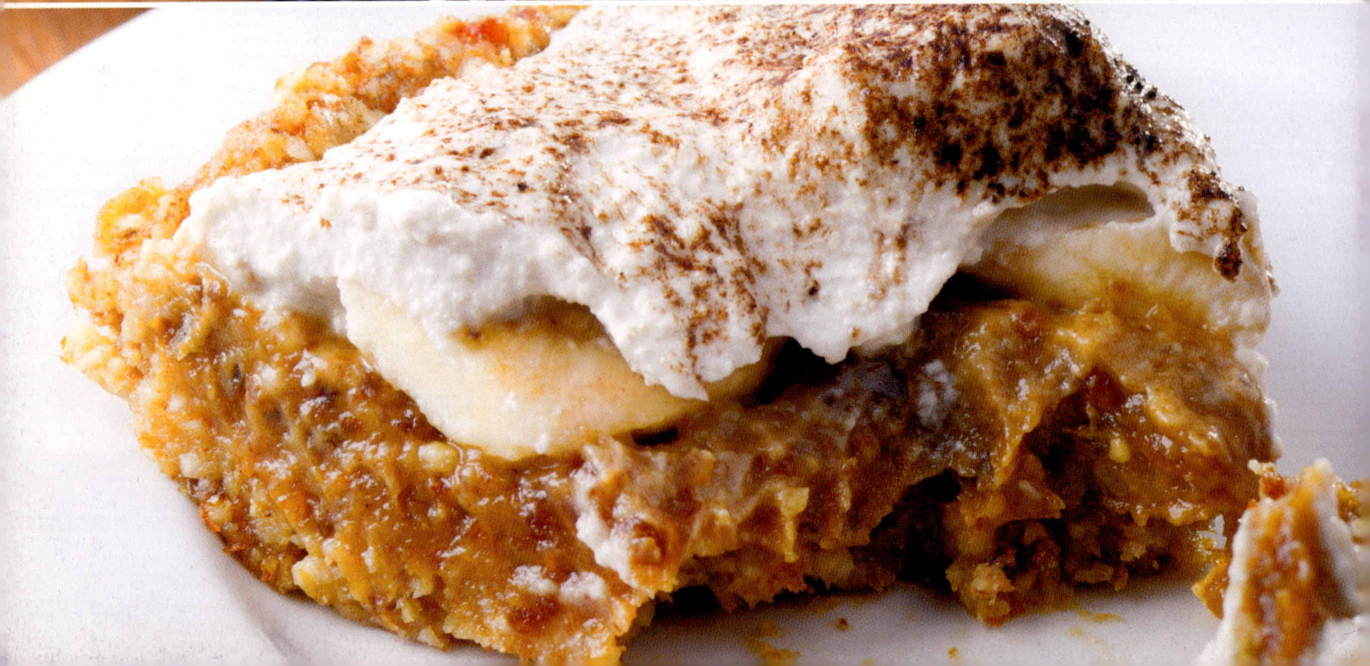

Step-by-Step

Mexican 180
Burgers 182
Dessert Pies 184

Use this step-by-step guide to help you customise your own recipes. Simply follow the instructions to create dishes based on your favourite ingredients and the ingredients you have available at the time.

Please note you will need a little cooking intelligence to make these work and the suggested serving sizes are a very rough guide. But give them a go and your cooking skills will quickly improve while you discover new dishes!

For other step-by-step guides see my first 3 books:

The Revive Cafe Cookbook 1	The Revive Cafe Cookbook 2	The Revive Cafe Cookbook 3
- Curries	- Soups	- Stuffed Veges
- Smoothies	- Breakfasts	- Dressings
- Salads	- Frittatas	- Wraps
- Stir Fries	- Dips	- Noodles
- Fritters	- Lasagnes	- Pizzas

Step-by-Step Mexican

A great way to enjoy some fresh healthy food

Just prepare a range of bowls of ingredients and let everyone make Mexican their own way!

1 Grain
cook or prepare

2 Protein
warm up

3 Fresh
prepare

---

choose 1:

cooked brown rice (page 186)

cooked quinoa (page 186)

coriander rice (page 134)

cooked bulghur wheat (page 186)

corn chips

tacos

---

choose 1:

black beans

chickpeas

pinto beans

fried tofu

---

choose 2:

cos (romaine) lettuce

tomato

red onion

fresh chilli

10,368 different combinations

4 Salsa
prepare

choose 1:

Mexican salsa (page 164)

corn fiesta (book 1, page 48)

pineapple salsa (book 1, page 48)

5 Dip
prepare

choose 1:

guacamole (page 177)

sunflower cream (book 1 page 146)

hummus (page 166, 177)

6 Extras
prepare

optional choose 1:

fried capsicum (bell peppers)

fried mushrooms

jalapenos

Step-by-Step Burgers

A great quick healthy lunch or meal - if you use whole-food ingredients!

Start with your healthy bread and just layer up all of the ingredients!

1. Bread — prepare

choose 1:

- whole grain bread
- whole grain burger bun
- whole grain foccacia bread

2. Protein — prepare

choose 1:

- Beefless Burgers (book 2 page 134)
- fried tofu slab (page 64)
- large portobello mushroom fried
- falafel (page 82)

3. Dressing — pour on

choose 1 or 2:

- satay sauce (page 90)
- Revive Aioli (page 174)
- southwestern dressing
- hummus (page 166, 177)
- plum sauce
- apricot sauce (page 60)
- Revive Relish (book 2 page 150)
- Cheezy Cashew Sauce (book 3 page 122)
- Mexican salsa (page 164)

10,497,600 *different combinations*

4 Fresh
prepare

choose 4:

large tomato slices

lettuce

sliced red onion

avocado slices

grated beetroot

grated carrot

5 Extras
put on

choose 1 or 2:

gherkins

sauerkraut

tinned beetroot

roasted pumpkin (butternut) slices

roasted kumara (sweet potato)

grilled or raw pineapple rings

Step-by-Step Dessert Pies

You can make some delicious desserts from whole food ingredients!

Choose a round 25cm (8in) dish and layer up the base, fillings, fruit, topping and garnish!

ROUGH GUIDE: Makes 12 servings

1 Base
process in food processor and press into dish

2 Filling
process in food processor and put on the base

3 Fruit
put on the top of the filling

---

use all:
- almonds
- cashew nuts
- dates (softened in water)

optional:
- rolled oats (oatmeal)
- linseeds
- sunflower seeds

---

choose 1 or 2:
- cashew nuts
- peanut butter
- tahini
- tofu
- avocado
- coconut milk

choose 1 sweetener:
- honey
- dates (softened in water)
- maple syrup
- carob powder

---

optional choose 1:
- banana sliced
- stewed rhubarb, apple
- tinned plums
- tinned apricots
- mango slices

20,072,448 *different combinations*

4 Topping
the top

choose 1 or 2:

sliced strawberries

blueberries

cashew cream

almond cream

sliced dried apricots

tinned apricot halves

sliced peaches

frozen berries cooked with arrowroot and water to form a glaze

5 Garnish
decorate on top

choose 1 or 2:

carob powder or nutmeg

shredded coconut

sesame seeds

mint leaves

chopped peanuts

chopped macadamia nuts

pumpkin seeds

lemon zest

honey

maple syrup

passionfruit pulp

Quick Guide Cooking Grains

Whole grains are high in fibre and nutrients. I prefer to cook them on the stove top.

Most grains yield approximately double their dry volume.

1. Boil water in your kettle - this will help cut time off the cooking process.
2. Put the required ratio of boiling water and grains into a pot at highest heat with the lid on.
3. Bring to the boil and then turn down and simmer (just bubbling). This is usually around ¼ heat setting.
4. Simmer for the required amount of time or until soft. If not quite cooked you can leave to sit with the lid on for another 10 minutes.
5. When the water reduces, steam vents will appear in the grains that assist with cooking. Do not stir as you will interrupt it.

Quick Guide Cooking Beans

Beans are high in protein. With a little planning, cooking your own beans is easy and you will save a lot of money.

These times are very approximate as the cooking time will vary significantly depending on the age and size of the bean.

1. Soak overnight (or at least 6 hours) in water (3 times as much water as beans).
2. Drain water and rinse in a colander or sieve.
3. Put fresh boiling water and beans into a pot and bring to boil. Simmer (just bubbling) on high heat for time specified or until soft.
4. Rinse under cold water in a colander or sieve.
5. Use straight away or put in refrigerator. Can be frozen and will defrost quickly under hot water.

Quick Guide Cooking Lentils

Lentils are high in protein and great in almost any savoury dish.

1. Lentils do not need soaking (except whole urid).
2. Bring to the boil with the amount of water indicated opposite and then turn down to simmer.
3. Cook with lid off for the approximate cooking times or until soft. Be careful as they can burn if water runs out.
4. Do not add salt until the end as this will inhibit the cooking process. Water will usually be used up but if not, drain.
5. Freeze any leftovers.

Long Grain Brown Rice - 1 cup
A great staple grain that I love to use. Ideal for serving with hotpots.

water: 2 cups | simmer: 30 minutes

Buck Wheat - 1 cup
A nice soft grain good for salads. Just add lots of flavour.

water: 2 cups | simmer: 20 minutes

Short Grain Brown Rice - 1 cup
Great for sticky rice salads, rice puddings and risottos.

water: 3 cups | simmer: 40 minutes

Fine Couscous - 1 cup
Don't cook! Just mix with boiling water, stir and let sit. Add turmeric for colour.

water: 1 cup | let sit: 5 minutes

Bulghur Wheat - 1 cup
Makes nice salads. Depending on the size, the time may vary.

water: 2 cups | simmer: 20 minutes

Quinoa - 1 cup
The perfect delicious, quick cooking grain. High in protein.

water: 2 cups | simmer: 12 minutes

Chickpeas - 1 cup
Our most used, favourite and delicious bean. Also called Garbanzo Beans.

water: 6 cups | simmer: 40 minutes

Black Beans - 1 cup
Nice in hotpots and salads for contrast. Also called Turtle Beans.

water: 6 cups | simmer: 30 minutes

Red Kidney Beans - 1 cup
Good all purpose bean. Great colour and holds its shape well.

water: 6 cups | simmer: 60 minutes

Large Lima Beans - 1 cup
Amazing in salads. Also called Butter Beans.

water: 6 cups | simmer: 60 minutes

Small White Beans - 1 cup
Good soft bean with a neutral flavour. Also called Navy Beans.

water: 6 cups | simmer: 60 minutes

Black-Eyed Beans - 1 cup
Nice in stews and hotpots.

water: 6 cups | simmer: 30 minutes

Red Lentils - 1 cup
A fast-cooking staple pantry item. Creates a delicious meal in minutes.

water: 3 cups | simmer: 10 minutes

Urid (Black) Lentils - 1 cup
Split urid are best. If whole you will need to soak overnight.

water: 6 cups | simmer: 50 minutes

Yellow Lentils - 1 cup
Like red lentils but with a more solid texture. Also called Toor Dahl.

water: 3 cups | simmer: 15 minutes

Brown (Crimson) Lentils - 1 cup
Great in lasagnes and casseroles. Nice with sage.

water: 3 cups | simmer: 30 minutes

French Green Lentils - 1 cup
Cook until just soft. They retain their shape. Also called Puy Lentils.

water: 4 cups | simmer: 40 minutes

Laird (Brown) Lentils - 1 cup
Often confused with brown lentils. These need a lot of flavour.

water: 3 cups | simmer: 30 minutes

The Revive Cafe Cookbook

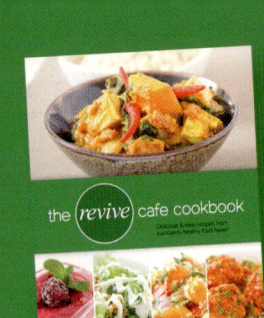

STEP BY STEP GUIDES:
Curries, Smoothies, Salads, Stir Fries, Fritters

Salads
- Cos Caesar 26
- Moroccan Chickpeas 28
- Seedy Slaw 30
- Classic Greek Salad 32
- Sweet Chilli Roast Veges 34
- Mushroom Risotto Salad 36
- Balsamic Lentil & Roasted Beetroot 38
- Italian Chickpeas 40
- Dukkah Roasted Potatoes 42
- Sweet Bean Medley 44
- Thai Green Curry Veges 46
- Corn & Pepper Fiesta 48
- Chewy Indonesian Rice 50
- Thai Satay Kumara Noodles 52
- Honey Mustard Roasted Potatoes 54
- Moroccan Leek Rice 56
- Almond Carrot Crunch 58
- Satay Cauliflower with Peanuts 60
- Spring Kumara Mingle 62
- Tuscan Mesclun 64
- Revive-dorf Salad 66
- Pacifika Coleslaw 68

Hotpots & Stir Fries
- Pumpkin, Spinach, Ginger & Tofu Curry 72
- Not Butter Chicken 74
- Corn & Potato Chowder 76
- Indonesian Chickpea Satay 78
- Thai Red Curry with Tofu 80
- Dahl Makhani 82
- Dahl-a-touille 84
- Malai Kofta 86
- Mushroom Bhaji 88
- Spanish Bean Stew 90
- Revive Chilli 92
- Mushroom Goulash 94
- Curried Cabbage Stir Fry 96
- Kidney Bean Stir Fry 98
- Quinoa Stir Fry 100
- Miso Bean Mingle 102
- Super Nachos 104

Main Meals
- Meatless Meatballs 108
- Not Chicken Burritos 110
- Baked Potato with Chickpea Korma 112
- Curried Zucchini Fritters 114
- Neat Loaf 116
- Honey & Soy Tofu Steaks 118
- Spanikopita 120
- Pumpkin Risotto Cake 122
- Pumpkin & Kumara Balls 124
- Mushroom Cannelloni 126
- Shepherdess Pie 128
- Indian Potato & Chickpea Wraps 130
- Scrambled Tofu with Mushrooms 132

Soups
- Carrot & Coriander Soup 136
- Creamy Tomato Soup 138
- Creamy Thai Pumpkin Soup 140
- Indian Spiced Lentil Soup 142

Flavour Boosters
- Sunflower Cream 146
- Classic Hummus 147
- Pineapple Salsa 148
- Almond Dukkah 149
- Revive Aioli 150
- Chermoula Dressing 151
- Satay Sauce 152
- Italian Tomato Sauce 153
- Date Puree 154
- Onion Jam 155

Sweet Things
- Boysenberry Nice-Cream 158
- Blueberry & Cashew Cheesecake 160
- Buckwheat Hotcakes w Pear Cream 162
- Apricot Oat Slice 164
- Blueberry Smoothie 166
- Banana Date Smoothie 167
- Boysenberry Rice Pudding 168
- 5 Grain Breakfast 170
- Bircher Muesli 172

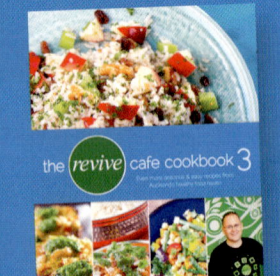

The Revive Cafe Cookbook 3

STEP BY STEP GUIDES:
Stuffed Veges, Dressings, Wraps, Noodles, Pizzas

Salads
- Brown Rice Waldorf 16
- Thai Ginger Slaw 18
- Mega Cos Salad 20
- Asian Ginger & Tofu Salad 22
- Autumn Cauliflower Mingle 24
- Blissful Sprout Medley 26
- Rainbow Chickpeas 28
- French Peanut Puy Lentils 30
- Olivier, The Russian Salad 32
- Sweet Shanghai Soy Beans 34
- Tangy Leafy Salad 36
- Italian Risotto 38
- Apple Poppy Coleslaw 40
- Caraway Kumara & Cabbage Salad 42
- Basil Linguine Salad 44
- Indian Curried Cauliflower & Chickpeas 46
- Fragrant Thai Peanut Noodles 48
- Quinoa & Cashew Mingle 50

Hotpots & Stir Fries
- Palak Paneer 54
- Penne Alfredo 56
- Thai Yellow Curry 58
- Peanutty Pineapple Quinoa 60
- Sweet & Sour Tofu 62
- Thai Massaman Lentil Casserole 64
- Cauliflower & Chickpea Satay 66
- Navratan Korma 68
- Mediterranean Quinoa & Sauce 70
- Italian Butter Bean Pasta 72
- Asparagus & Quinoa Stir Fry 74
- Steam Fried Veges 76
- Donburi 78

Main Meals
- Scrummy Stuffed Sweet Potato 82
- Kumara & Carrot Cakes 84
- Pumpkin & Cranberry Filo Parcels 86
- Okonomiyaki (Japanese Pancake) 88
- Vegetable Pakoras 90
- Broccoli Infused Flatbread 92
- Summer Burger 94
- Smoked Stuffed Peppers 96
- Pesto & Potato Chickbread Pizza 98
- Courgette & Cauliflower Bake 100
- Thai Spring Rolls 102

Soups
- Mexican Black Bean Soup 108
- Vietnamese Pho Noodles 110
- Lentil & Beetroot Borscht 112
- Broccoli & Dill Soup 114
- Lentil & Kumara Soup 116
- Leek & Potato Soup 118

Flavour Boosters
- Cheezy Cashew Sauce 122
- Basil Hummus 124
- Nutty Capsicum Dip 124
- Sparkling Lime Juice 126
- Almost Egg Spread 128
- Thai Ginger Dressing 130
- Tofu Mayo 132
- Almond Butter 133

Breakfasts
- Power Oat Breakfast 138
- Nearly French Toast 140
- Warming Millet Porridge 142
- Buckwheat Waffles 144
- Butternut Oatmeal 146
- Golden Omelette 148
- Portobello Mushrooms 150

Sweet Things
- Plum & Ginger Slice 154
- Apricot Bliss Balls 156
- Better Than Ice Cream 158
- Pineapple Rice Pudding 160
- Black Almond Fudge 162
- Peanut Butter Smoothie 164
- Blueberry, Apple Crumble 166
- Pumpkin Pie 168
- Honest Pina Colada 170
- Banana Split 172
- Coconut & Date Fudge 174

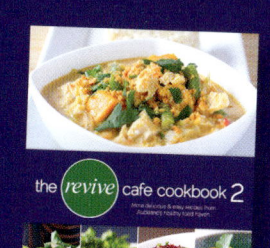

STEP BY STEP GUIDES:
Soups, Breakfasts, Frittatas, Dips, Lasagnes

Salads

4C Salad 18
Sesame Asian Greens 20
Spiced Date Pilau 22
Revive Raw Salad 24
Cos & Courgette Mingle 26
Thai Satay Noodles 28
Israeli Couscous 30
Creamy Roasted Veges 32
Smoked Spanish Rice 34
Egyptian Rice & Lentils 36

Thai Bean Mingle 38
Pad Thai Noodle Salad 40
Bombay Roasted Potatoes 42
Mesclun Mango 44
Italian Fusilli Mingle 46
Green Salad & Almonds 48
Summer Quinoa Mingle 50
Pesto Infused Roasted Potatoes 52
Wild Green Salad 54
Greek Chickpeas 56
Italian Pumpkin Risotto 58
Kumara & Cranberry Mingle 60
Curried Black-Eyed Bean Salad 62
Baghdad Bulghur 64
Pesto Penne Pasta 66
Creamy Thai Rice Salad 68
Brussels Sprout Medley 70

Hotpots & Stir Fries

Indonesian Sadur Lodeh 74
Classic Chickpea Ratatouille 76
Thai Tofu Green Curry 78
Not Chicken Alfredo 80
Mixed Bean Jumbalaya 82
Tofu & Quinoa Stir Fry 84
Moroccan Date & Chickpea Dahl 86
Curried Poppy Seed Dahl 88

Indian Spinach & Chickpea Korma 90
Tarka Dahl 92
Hearty Lentil Casserole 94
Chilli Con Tofu 96
Thai Massaman Peanut Curry 98
Thai Green Curry Lentils 100
Italian White Bean Stew 102
Tuscan Brown Lentils 104
Asian Peanut Stir Fry 106
Mediterranean Chickpea Stir Fry 108
Herbed Lentil & Quinoa Stir Fry 110
Indian Rice Pilaf 112

Main Meals

Baked Thai Corn Cakes 116
Tuscan White Bean Wraps 118
Revive Roast Vege Frittata 120
Greek Potato & Feta Cake 122
Thai Tofu Curry Pie 124
Lentil & Vegetable Lasagne 126
Curried Potato Cakes 128
Indian Curried Filo Pie 130
Chickpea Pizza 132
Beefless Burgers 134
Tuscan White Bean Cannelloni 136

Traditional Corn Fritters 138

Flavour Boosters

Healthy Basil Pesto 142
Chick Bread 144
Avocado Guacamole 146
Root-beet Dip 148
Red Pepper Pesto 149
Revive Relish 150
White Cashew Sauce 152
Tomato Salsa 153
Ravishing Red Bean Dip 154

Sweet Things

Bliss Balls 160
Revive Muesli (Granola) 162
Whipped Cashew Cream 164
Classic Strawberry Smoothie 165
Almond Milk 166
Boysenberry Smoothie 168
Tropical Fruit Salad 169
Hot Honey, Lemon & Ginger Soother 170
Porridge (Oatmeal) 172
Mango Smoothie 174
Carob Ice 175
Muesli Smoothie 176

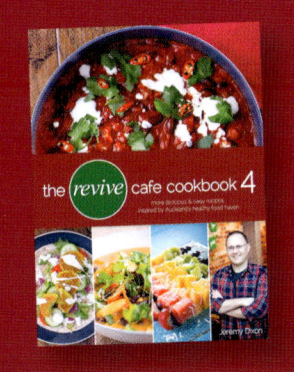

STEP BY STEP GUIDES:
Mexican, Burgers, Dessert Pies

Salads

Fresh Autumn Mingle 16
Asian Quinoa Salad 18
Root Vegetable Medley 20
Asian Soba Noodles 22
Watercress & Sweet Potato 24
Tempeh & Cherry Tomato 26
Cauli-cous Salad 28
Leek & Pesto Chickpeas 30
Kale & Lentil Salad 32
Succotash 34
German Roasted Potatoes 36

Fruity Moroccan Couscous 38
Quick Tahini Coleslaw 40
Italian Tomato Rice Salad 42
Summer Spiral Pasta Salad 44
Sesame Cucumber Ribbon 46

Hotpots & Stir Fries

Chilli Con Haba 52
Aromatic Cambodian Curry 54
Tuscan Bean Casserole 56
Penang Thai Bean Curry 58
Sweet Apricot Sesame Tofu 60
Super-charged Lentil Stew 62
Thai Almond Tofu Noodles 64
Mushroom & Cashew Rice 66
Figgy Thai Chickpeas 68
Black Bean Stir Fry 70
Thai Green Curry Stir Fry 72
Mexican Quinoa 74
Cambodian Red Rice 76

Main Meals

Falafel Pita Wraps 82
Creamed Corn Baked Potato 84
Turkish Moussaka 86
Energising Mexican Feast 88
Satay Tofu Kebabs 90
Tamale Pie 92
Thai Infused Baked Potatoes 94

Reuben Burger 96
Mushroom & Leek Risotto 98

Soups

Chunky Vegetable & Lentil 102
Creamy & Minty Pea Soup 104
Mushroom & Thyme Soup 106
Satay Sweet Potato Bisque 108
Minestrone 110
Malaysian Laksa 112
Curried Cauliflower Soup 114

Sides

Mediterranean Vegetables 120
Honey Glazed Carrots 122
Traditional Potato Mash 123
Sweet Potato Fries 124
Garlic Mushrooms 126
Broccoli & Cranberries 127
Satay Green Beans 128
Smoked Wedges 130
Green Pea Mingle 131
Cauliflower Cheese 132
Tangy Coriander Rice 134
Roasted Beetroot 135
Breakfast Vegetables 136

Sweet Things

Blueberry Parfait 140

Rainbow Fruit Kebabs 142
Healthy Banoffee Pie 144
Sticky Rice Mango 146
Chewy Cranberry Oat Slice 148
Blueberries & Cashew 150
Jeremy's Quinoa Breakfast 152
Moorish Carrot Cake Balls 154
Not Chocolate Mousse 156
Raspberry & Mint Smoothie 158
Sublime Green Smoothie 160
Mango & Lime Shake 161

Flavour Boosters

Mexican Salsa 164
Asian Sesame Miso 165
Moroccan Hummus 166
Homemade Sweet Chilli 168
Baba Ganoush 170
Tahini Dressing 171
Thai Red Curry Paste 172
Thai Green Curry Paste 173
Revive Aioli 174
Italian Tomato Sauce 174
Basil Pesto 175
Date Puree 175
Tofu Mayo 176
Cashew Cream 176
Classic Hummus 177
Avocado Guacamole 177

Recipe Index

A
Aioli, Revive 174
Almond Tofu Noodles, Thai 64
Apricot Sesame Tofu, Sweet 60
Aromatic Cambodian Tofu Curry 54
Asian Quinoa Salad 18
Asian Sesame Miso Dressing 165
Asian Soba Noodles 22
Autumn Mingle, Fresh 16
Avocado Guacamole 177

B
Baba Ganoush 170
Baked Potato, Creamed Corn 84
Baked Potatoes, Thai Infused 94
Balls, Moorish Carrot Cake 154
Banoffee Pie, Healthy 144
Basil Pesto 175
Bean Casserole, Tuscan Three 56
Bean Curry, Penang Thai 58
Beans, Satay Green 128
Bean Stir Fry, Black 70
Beetroot, Roasted 135
Bisque, Satay Sweet Potato 108
Black Bean Stir Fry 70
Blueberries & Cashew Cream 150
Blueberry Parfait 140
Breakfast, Jeremy's Fast Quinoa 152
Breakfast Vegetables 136
Broccoli & Cranberries 127
Buckwheat Risotto, Mushroom & Leek 98
Burger, Reuben 96
Butternut Hummus, Moroccan 166

C
Cake Balls, Moorish Carrot 154
Cambodian Red Rice 76
Cambodian Tofu Curry, Aromatic 54
Carrot Cake Balls, Moorish 154
Carrots, Honey Glazed 122
Cashew Cream 176
Cashew Cream, Blueberries & 150
Cashew Fried Rice, Mushroom & 66
Casserole, Tuscan Three Bean 56
Cauli-cous Salad 28
Cauliflower Cheese 132
Cauliflower Soup, Curried 114
Cheese, Cauliflower 132
Cherry Tomato Salad, Tempeh & 26
Chewy Cranberry Oat Slice 148
Chickpeas, Figgy Thai 68
Chickpeas, Leek & Pesto 30
Chilli Con Haba 52
Chilli Sauce, Homemade Sweet 168
Chocolate Mousse, Not 156
Chunky Vegetable & Lentil Soup 102
Classic Hummus 177
Coleslaw, Quick Tahini 40
Coriander Rice, Tangy 134
Corn Baked Potato, Creamed 84
Couscous, Fruity Moroccan 38
Cranberries, Broccoli & 127
Cranberry Oat Slice, Chewy 148
Cream, Blueberries & Cashew 150
Cream, Cashew 176
Creamed Corn Baked Potato 84
Creamy & Minty Pea Soup 104
Cucumber Ribbon Salad, Sesame 46
Curried Cauliflower Soup 114
Curry, Aromatic Cambodian Tofu 54
Curry Paste, Homemade Thai Green 173
Curry Paste, Homemade Thai Red 172
Curry, Penang Thai Bean 58
Curry Stir Fry, Thai Green 72

D
Date Puree 175
Dressing, Asian Sesame Miso 165
Dressing, Tahini 171

E
Energising Mexican Feast 88

F
Falafel Pita Wraps 82
Fast Quinoa Breakfast, Jeremy's 152
Feast, Energising Mexican 88
Figgy Thai Chickpeas 68
Fresh Autumn Mingle 16
Fried Rice, Mushroom & Cashew 66
Fries, Sweet Potato 124
Fruit Kebabs, Rainbow 142
Fruity Moroccan Couscous 38

G
Garlic Mushrooms 126
German Roasted Potatoes 36
Glazed Carrots, Honey 122
Green Beans, Satay 128
Green Curry Paste, Homemade Thai 173
Green Curry Stir Fry, Thai 72
Green Pea Mingle 131
Green Smoothie, Sublime 160
Guacamole, Avocado 177

H
Haba, Chilli Con 52
Healthy Banoffee Pie 144
Homemade Sweet Chilli Sauce 168
Homemade Thai Green Curry Paste 173
Homemade Thai Red Curry Paste 172
Honey Glazed Carrots 122
Hummus, Classic 177
Hummus, Moroccan Butternut 166

I
Italian Tomato Rice Salad 42
Italian Tomato Sauce 174

J
Jeremy's Fast Quinoa Breakfast 152

K
Kale & Lentil Salad 32
Kebabs, Rainbow Fruit 142
Kebabs, Satay Tofu 90

L
Laksa, Malaysian 112
Leek Buckwheat Risotto, Mushroom & 98
Leek & Pesto Chickpeas 30
Lentil Salad, Kale & 32
Lentil Soup, Chunky Vegetable & 102
Lentil Stew, Super-charged 62
Lime Shake, Mango & 161

M
Malaysian Laksa 112
Mango & Lime Shake 161
Mango, Sticky Rice 146

Mash, Traditional Potato 123
Mayo, Tofu 176
Mediterranean Vegetables 120
Medley, Root Vegetable 20
Mexican Feast, Energising 88
Mexican Quinoa 74
Mexican Salsa 164
Minestrone 110
Mingle, Fresh Autumn 16
Mingle, Green Pea 131
Mint Smoothie, Raspberry & 158
Minty Pea Soup, Creamy & 104
Miso Dressing, Asian Sesame 165
Moorish Carrot Cake Balls 154
Moroccan Butternut Hummus 166
Moroccan Couscous, Fruity 38
Moussaka, Turkish 86
Mousse, Not Chocolate 156
Mushroom & Cashew Fried Rice 66
Mushroom & Leek Buckwheat Risotto 98
Mushrooms, Garlic 126
Mushroom & Thyme Soup 106

N

Noodles, Asian Soba 22
Noodles, Thai Almond Tofu 64
Not Chocolate Mousse 156

O

Oat Slice, Chewy Cranberry 148

P

Parfait, Blueberry 140
Pasta Salad, Summer Spiral 44
Pea Mingle, Green 131
Pea Soup, Creamy & Minty 104
Penang Thai Bean Curry 58
Pesto, Basil 175
Pesto Chickpeas, Leek & 30
Pie, Healthy Banoffee 144
Pie, Tamale 92
Pita Wraps, Falafel 82
Potato, Creamed Corn Baked 84
Potatoes, German Roasted 36
Potatoes, Thai Infused Baked 94
Potato Mash, Traditional 123
Puree, Date 175

Q

Quick Tahini Coleslaw 40
Quinoa Breakfast, Jeremy's Fast 152

Quinoa, Mexican 74
Quinoa Salad, Asian 18

R

Rainbow Fruit Kebabs 142
Raspberry & Mint Smoothie 158
Red Curry Paste, Homemade Thai 172
Red Rice, Cambodian 76
Reuben Burger 96
Revive Aioli 174
Ribbon Salad, Sesame Cucumber 46
Rice, Cambodian Red 76
Rice Mango, Sticky 146
Rice, Mushroom & Cashew Fried 66
Rice Salad, Italian Tomato 42
Rice, Tangy Coriander 134
Risotto, Mushroom & Leek Buckwheat 98
Roasted Beetroot 135
Roasted Potatoes, German 36
Root Vegetable Medley 20

S

Salad, Asian Quinoa 18
Salad, Cauli-cous 28
Salad, Italian Tomato Rice 42
Salad, Kale & Lentil 32
Salad, Sesame Cucumber Ribbon 46
Salad, Summer Spiral Pasta 44
Salad, Tempeh & Cherry Tomato 26
Salad, Watercress & Sweet Potato 24
Salsa, Mexican 164
Satay Green Beans 128
Satay Sweet Potato Bisque 108
Satay Tofu Kebabs 90
Sauce, Italian Tomato 174
Sesame Cucumber Ribbon Salad 46
Sesame Miso Dressing, Asian 165
Sesame Tofu, Sweet Apricot 60
Shake, Mango & Lime 161
Slice, Chewy Cranberry Oat 148
Smoked Wedges 130
Smoothie, Raspberry & Mint 158
Smoothie, Sublime Green 160
Soba Noodles, Asian 22
Soup, Chunky Vegetable & Lentil 102
Soup, Creamy & Minty Pea 104
Soup, Curried Cauliflower 114
Soup, Mushroom & Thyme 106
Spiral Pasta Salad, Summer 44
Stew, Super-charged Lentil 62
Sticky Rice Mango 146

Stir Fry, Black Bean 70
Stir Fry, Thai Green Curry 72
Sublime Green Smoothie 160
Succotash 34
Summer Spiral Pasta Salad 44
Super-charged Lentil Stew 62
Sweet Apricot Sesame Tofu 60
Sweet Chilli Sauce, Homemade 168
Sweet Potato Bisque, Satay 108
Sweet Potato Fries 124
Sweet Potato Salad, Watercress & 24

T

Tahini Coleslaw, Quick 40
Tahini Dressing 171
Tamale Pie 92
Tangy Coriander Rice 134
Tempeh & Cherry Tomato Salad 26
Thai Almond Tofu Noodles 64
Thai Bean Curry, Penang 58
Thai Chickpeas, Figgy 68
Thai Green Curry Paste, Homemade 173
Thai Green Curry Stir Fry 72
Thai Infused Baked Potatoes 94
Thai Red Curry Paste, Homemade 172
Three Bean Casserole, Tuscan 56
Thyme Soup, Mushroom & 106
Tofu Curry, Aromatic Cambodian 54
Tofu Kebabs, Satay 90
Tofu Mayo 176
Tofu Noodles, Thai Almond 64
Tofu, Sweet Apricot Sesame 60
Tomato Rice Salad, Italian 42
Tomato Sauce, Italian 174
Traditional Potato Mash 123
Turkish Moussaka 86
Tuscan Three Bean Casserole 56

V

Vegetable & Lentil Soup, Chunky 102
Vegetable Medley, Root 20
Vegetables, Breakfast 136
Vegetables, Mediterranean 120

W

Watercress & Sweet Potato Salad 24
Wedges, Smoked 130
Wraps, Falafel Pita 82